Psychoanalytic Group Psychotherapy

In this comprehensive volume, Richard M. Billow provides a thorough introduction to group psychotherapy from a psychoanalytic perspective.

Billow integrates contemporary psychoanalytic thinking with Freudian and Kleinian core concepts, as well as Bion's early group theory and his later metapsychology, to provide a holistic overview of group therapy and its potential benefits for patients. He incorporates major psychoanalytic thinkers outside the American relational mainstream – such as Lacan, Laplanche, Kaes, Foulkes, and Pichon Riviere, as well as his own prominent contributions to the field – to provide a unique and interdisciplinary overview. Throughout the chapters, readers will be introduced to challenging clinical experiences that illustrate some of the similarities and differences among psychoanalytic and other psychodynamic group approaches. Offering guidelines on how to harness and conduct the group, Billow provides exceptional insight into the veritable benefits of maintaining an analytic stance within the clinical setting.

Written in a clear and accessible style, this book is a vital tool for students and professionals interested in a thorough overview of psychoanalytically-based group treatments.

Richard M. Billow is a clinical psychologist based in New York, USA. He was the director of the Postgraduate Group Program at the Derner Institute, Adelphi University, New York and currently serves as Clinical Professor in Adelphi's Postgraduate Programs in Psychoanalysis and Psychotherapy. He is the author of *Relational Group Psychotherapy: From Basic Assumptions to Passion* (2003), *Resistance, Rebellion and Refusal in Groups: The 3 Rs* (2010), *Developing Nuclear Ideas: Relational Group Psychotherapy* (2015), and *Richard M. Billow's Selected Papers on Psychoanalysis and Group Process: Changing Our Minds* (T. Slonim, Ed., 2021).

Routledge Introductions to Contemporary Psychoanalysis

Series Editor: Aner Govrin
Executive Editor: Yael Peri Herzovich

This comprehensive series illuminates the intricate landscape of psychoanalytic theory and practice. In this collection of concise yet illuminating volumes, we delve into the influential figures, groundbreaking concepts, and transformative theories that shape the contemporary psychoanalytic landscape. At the heart of each volume lies a commitment to clarity, accessibility, and depth. Our expert authors, renowned scholars and practitioners in their respective fields, guide readers through the complexities of psychoanalytic thought with precision and enthusiasm. Whether you are a seasoned psychoanalyst, a student eager to explore the field, or a curious reader seeking insight into the human psyche, our series offers a wealth of knowledge and insight.

The Evidence for Psychodynamic Psychotherapy
A Contemporary Introduction
Kevin McCarthy, Carla Capone and Liat Liebovich

Psychoanalytic Group Psychotherapy
A Contemporary Introduction
Richard M. Billow

Existential Psychoanalysis
A Contemporary Introduction
M. Guy Thompson

For more information about this series, please visit:
www. https://www.routledge.com/Routledge-Introductions-to-Contemporary-Psychoanalysis/book-series/ICP

Psychoanalytic Group Psychotherapy

A Contemporary Introduction

Richard M. Billow

LONDON AND NEW YORK

Designed cover image: © Michal Heiman, Asylum 1855–2020, *The Sleeper* (video, psychoanalytic sofa and Plate 34), exhibition view, Herzliya Museum of Contemporary Art, 2017

First published 2025
by Routledge
4 Park Square, Milton Park, Abingdon, Oxon OX14 4RN

and by Routledge
605 Third Avenue, New York, NY 10158

Routledge is an imprint of the Taylor & Francis Group, an informa business

© 2025 Richard M. Billow

The right of Richard M. Billow to be identified as author[/s] of this work has been asserted in accordance with sections 77 and 78 of the Copyright, Designs and Patents Act 1988.

All rights reserved. No part of this book may be reprinted or reproduced or utilised in any form or by any electronic, mechanical, or other means, now known or hereafter invented, including photocopying and recording, or in any information storage or retrieval system, without permission in writing from the publishers.

Trademark notice: Product or corporate names may be trademarks or registered trademarks, and are used only for identification and explanation without intent to infringe.

British Library Cataloguing-in-Publication Data
A catalogue record for this book is available from the British Library

ISBN: 978-1-032-70323-7 (hbk)
ISBN: 978-1-032-68606-6 (pbk)
ISBN: 978-1-032-70325-1 (ebk)

DOI: 10.4324/9781032703251

Typeset in Times New Roman
by Taylor & Francis Books

To new generations of group therapists, and to my grandchildren, Jordyn, Jaxon, and Mason Leibowitz, and Syenna Billow. Grow, prosper, spread knowledge and good cheer.

Contents

Acknowledgments		ix
Introduction: Organization of the Book		x

PART I
Overview   1

1	Making Sense of The Group Experience	3
2	How is Group Psychotherapy Psychoanalytic?	11
3	Genealogy	16

PART II
Core Concepts   37

4	The Expanded Psychoanalytic Group Frame	39
5	Group Process	53
6	Vertical and Horizontal Vectors	69

PART III
Doing Our Work   79

7	Impasses and Opportunities	81

8 The Group as a Psychoanalytic Object   105

   References   126
   Index   141

Acknowledgments

Generations of senior clinicians, colleagues, students, patients, and journal editors have given needed access to the creative minds of many others. Dr. Aner Govrin guided me through the development of this volume, along with fruitful discussions with Drs. Earl Hopper and Joseph Newirth. Productive exchanges with Dr. Tzachi Slonim, who organized and annotated my *Selected Papers* (Routledge, 2021), provided an integrative frame that I carry forward. Dr. Charles Raps has shared and greatly contributed to my writing career. His job as uber editor has been supplemented by the fine editorial instincts of Dr. Hilary Callan Curtis. My wife, Elyse, children, Jennifer, David, and Brette, and their spouses Bryon and Winnie, have kept me sane and centered.

Introduction: Organization of the Book

This book is designed for a diverse audience: people interested in becoming or ready to become group practitioners, curious readers seeking to expand their knowledge about group dynamics, and those who want to learn more about group therapy in general. It offers clarity and guidelines regarding the similarities and differences among contemporary psychodynamic approaches, making it valuable for both professionals and laypeople interested in the field. Whether you are a practitioner-in-training, a curious observer, or someone looking to deepen their understanding, this book provides insights into the complexities and nuances of psychodynamic group psychotherapy. In doing the research and reading or rereading the major theoreticians and creators of texts in our field, I realized that I too was benefitting from this cohering review.

While not a "how to" text, my expectation is that with a clearer understanding of the various ways we may think about group psychotherapy, the therapist will more comfortably ease into the work. Since this book presents an introduction to *psychoanalytic* group therapy as well, I describe recent developments in psychoanalytic ideas that are relevant to the individual therapist and group therapist alike. To approach the work psychoanalytically, we need to think psychoanalytically. This requires establishing and maintaining what Bion referred to as the "*psychoanalytic function of the personality*," an idea introduced in *Chapter 1* and relevant both to the therapist and group members; really, to all individuals.

Here are brief descriptions of each chapter. In *Part I: Overview, Chapter 1, Making Sense of The Group Experience* situates the reader within the group experience, so as to get a sense of how it might feel to lead a group. I designate some of the anxieties and dreads that accompany us and our resistances to group, no matter how much we might desire the experience. The chapter concludes with a discussion of my integrative approach, key influencers, and the goals I seek to achieve in this volume and in clinical work.

Chapter 2, How is Group Psychotherapy Psychoanalytic? describes conflicting institutional attitudes towards psychoanalytic group psychotherapy – represented by Freud and Bion – and the specific qualities of a *psychoanalytic* group. These include focus on transference–countertransference, the recognition of repression (and dissociation) and resistance, and the importance of sexuality and of the Oedipus Complex (triangular relationships).

Chapter 3, Genealogy, is dedicated to mapping of the field. Three broad historic models – the Freudian–Kleinian psychoanalytic, interpersonal, and group dynamic (group as a whole) – clarify key differences and the many overlaps among them. I reclassify and add to these historical and foundational categories to integrate subsequent developments in group theory and practice.

In *Part II, Core Concepts, Chapter 4, The Expanded Group Frame* broaches many topics: membership criteria; advantages of combined treatment; revised concepts of confidentiality, anonymity, naturality, and abstinence; self-disclosure; free association and group discourse; words, action, and enaction; transference-countertransference; reality testing and testing reality; aggression in conflict and growth models; and unrepresented and unrepresentable states.

Chapter 5, Group Process considers group forces ("*G*") and phases; conceptual and experiential categories the therapist brings to a group; and the interplay between *internal groups* and *actual groups, primary* and *secondary process, psychotic* and *normal/neurotic positions*, and among *basic affects* of loving, hating, and curiosity (*LHK*). Configurations of *resistance, rebellion*, and *refusal* designate how individuals and groups cope with the therapeutic project. Whether relatively passive, active, or interpretive, the group therapist remains a central figure. To some extent, it is "*all about me*," the therapist.

Chapter 6, Vertical and Horizontal Vectors shows how siblings are always part of therapeutic process. Much of what the group struggles with lies outside the realm of the here-and-now intersubjective matrix and relates to early sibling relationships. An arguably unique feature of group psychotherapy is access to the here-and-now psychic reality of siblings. Freud's "sibling complex" may account for traditional psychanalysis' neglect of psychoanalytic group therapy. Kaës' "dual axes" theory – interacting early Oedipal and sibling dynamics – provides a valuable perspective on group structure and process. I retranscribe Bion's "*container–contained*" to include a sibling vector.

In *Part III, Doing Our Work, Chapter 7, Impasses and Opportunities* presents Bion's metapsychological rubric of thinking, factual truth, psychic truth, and "falsity." Especially in aroused states of perceived threat and confrontation, individuals, groups, and larger social and political organizations tend to resort to *fixed narratives, irruptions*, and *polarized* thinking and behavior. To resolve these short or longer-term impasses, the group therapist must challenge hardening attitudes and antagonisms and contain *irruptive reactions* without being unduly jarring or appearing unempathic. I describe two complementary models of seizing therapeutic opportunity: Bion's seminal "*container–contained*" and my "*four strategies of therapeutic discourse.*" These denote modes of conceptualizing, listening, and speaking as the group cycles through the inevitable processes of *resistance, rebellion*, and *refusal*. Taking *entitlements* as leader, the therapist navigates these modes to cement bonding, build trust, reduce falsity, and allow symbolic, as well as actual, relationships to evolve.

Chapter 8, The Group as a Psychoanalytic Object defines Bion's concept of the *psychoanalytic object* and Billow's group-adaptive *nuclear idea*. They provide a conceptual framework to view events through a common interpretive lens, treating all participants as tangible beings and also as representatives of *emotional ideas*. Claiming Freud as our profession's premier deconstructionist, I illustrate how the group leader's words, deeds, and presence furthers the essential psychoanalytic process of *deconstruction/reconstruction*. In contrast to accenting here-and-now interactions and rapid shifts of attention from one member to another, the deconstructive–reconstructive process needs time and reflective space. And always, the psychoanalytic project demands the therapist's loving, curious attitude and appreciative receptivity to others, but also, access to feelings of irritation, confusion, and unknowing. The chapter summarizes the author's relational stance and concludes with remarks about a relationally-informed, group psychoanalytic psychotherapy.

Part I

Overview

Chapter 1

Making Sense of The Group Experience

Group psychotherapy can make analysts "shudder," as one of its founders, S. H. Foulkes (1964, p. 125), declared. "Everybody and nobody is a therapist, everybody and nobody a patient." Any therapist contemplating starting a group – the novice, traditionally trained psychoanalysts, and even long-time practitioners – may shudder at facing the additional pitfalls and crises that this challenging treatment offers. Unlike the dyadic set-up with the therapist as the benevolently singular other, in group, there are many others, whose presences are neither dispassionate nor necessarily collaborative. We have less control, more self-exposure, and more risk, which are the very reasons that make group work compelling. We hone our craft in every session.

The beginner may take solace: like veteran actors, seasoned group therapists do not lose stage fright. Anxiety, transference, and resistance are basic and continuous in the therapist, intensely more so in the group. All participants are "habitually under the sway of group formation" (Freud, 1921, p. 123). What is real, imagined, truly significant, and of potential therapeutic value? The therapist ponders, steadfast in the conviction that a group can reach unequaled maturational goals. "It's true, it's old, and it's unreachable; it's a barrier for me," a member lamented. How can the leader direct the group towards the unreachable? To ease *unnecessary* shuddering and increase the likelihood of growth-producing, lively emotional experiences, this volume offers ways of looking at the group entity, group process, membership, and the therapist's co-participation.

Consider our Position as Group Therapists

In each session we are faced with the pressure of understanding what is occurring and deciding what to say, when, and to whom. Whether we talk or remain silent, we are continually observed and assert influence. Our interventions reach many individuals simultaneously, yet they are heard differently. Ideally, they should be experience-near and context-relevant, reflect our relationship with each group member and advance his or her growth, access unconscious group and individual processes, and, further, have sociopolitical and metapsychological depth. They should serve multiple purposes, but not be at cross-purposes; usefully ambiguous and thought provoking, but not needlessly confusing and confounding. Interventions can be comforting and anxiety arousing simultaneously, without being falsely reassuring or fear inducing. We want interventions to be powerful but not subdue the members' freedom to generate and shape group process.

Our essential task is to establish an environment to utilize ourselves, members, and whole group to foster meaning-making and emotional growth. In my opinion, what holds a productive group together is the therapist's ever-expanding understanding of the psychic realities of the group and its members, and the therapist's success in interesting others in reaching and deepening such understanding, however painful and unwelcome.

The Therapist's Anxiety and Resistance to Group

Symbolically, psychodynamic therapy is an act of aggression, since it interferes, challenges, and undermines an individual's fixed beliefs, values, and relationships, and possibly one's sense of self (see *Chapter 7* on *deconstruction*). I suggest that in thinking of group, prospective and current members unconsciously, and often consciously, feel the therapist is abandoning, exiling, and hating them by limiting an exclusive relationship and exposing them to others. The therapist also feels this to be so and endures anxiety and guilt. In addition, like others, the therapist suffers abandonment anxieties and fears exposure. The group situation – and not the nature of learning – comes to represent the source of danger.

The therapist hates and dreads the group for subjecting him or her to the very group one has longed for and created!

> A skilled analyst who tended to be quiet and reserved insisted that she did not have the personality to run a group. "I'm a follower, not a leader," she insisted, "I can't think that quickly when I'm under pressure." I did not believe "leading," meaning quickly responding, was a job requirement. A quiet, reflective leader who takes her time can be quite effective in containing anxiety and encouraging the evolutionary process of learning. Bion wrote about nonverbal containment: how the therapist's capacity for "reverie" (dream-like, internal free-associations), patience, and inner security communicate something crucially important, even curative, furthering the group members' capacity to tolerate powerful affects and develop emotional thoughts. In exploring this woman's history, we discovered that in her former occupation as a teacher, she led others quite capably. She also valued her own experience in group therapy, in which she came to actively participate. However, she adamantly maintained her belief that, as a group therapist, she would retreat to the unconfident role she had occupied in her originary family and which could re-emerge in certain social situations. She did not feel able to offer her patients what she considered a valuable option.

I asked advanced candidates in our Adelphi Group Program how their first groups were going. They looked forward to each session with excitement and dread:

> 1. [From a male candidate] "I was having trouble. Two of the four women dropped out, and I felt responsible for bringing in a female member who would stick, although the group seemed okay either way. I had this dream the night before introducing a new woman: My [male] supervisor, the men in the group, and I were holding hands, in a circle. I think I felt I was falling apart, and I needed the other men to keep me together."

2. "I get scared that people will fight with each other, so scared that I feel I wouldn't be coherent if I had to talk. I feel like I can't focus or process. I hear 'fix it' in my head, but I have no idea what to do. I drive myself so crazy that the room can spin around."

3. "My mind can go blank, yet I will feel a painful imploding inside it. I can get up after a difficult session so uncoordinated I don't know where my feet are. At the same time. I can't wait for the next session and already want to start another group."

4. "I can feel a grudge towards patients who won't join my group. They don't know what's good for them...for me."

In anticipating a new group, the therapist affixes on a vague entity, a group-as-fetus. And, upon entering the first session, the group becomes the baby born. Perhaps the most difficult, and saddest, aspect of the therapist's job is to separate sufficiently from this neonatal group to become its leader. While the group struggles with babyhood, to maintain connection, and to feel secure, the leader struggles with parenthood and feeling adequate. Will I deliver a healthy, truth-seeking group? Can I adequately nurture such a group and challenge the group's inherent antagonism to what it needs? Will the group love me?

The therapist must believe that what is special and caring in individual psychoanalytic treatment will not be lost in a group, but will be enhanced by the presence of others. How will members respond to the therapist's "group family?" An anxious therapist may unnecessarily shepherd members through the inclusion and absorption phase, behaving like "an over-careful parent who discusses all possibilities with the patient, as a mother would with a child going on a long trip when she thinks he cannot tackle possible difficulties" (Koenig and Lindner, 1994, p. 123). When members integrate, the therapist may feel suddenly useless, like an unneeded parent. And let's not forget the unappetizing reality that the inclusion process often involves attempts to *increase* the therapist's anxiety, as members redirect anger towards their new "siblings" to the motives and foibles of their leader.

Activating the "psychoanalytic function of the personality"

Freud mythologized an antagonism between the pleasure and reality principles, and between the life and death instincts. Klein narrated dynamic interplays between love and hate, and envy and reparative gratitude. Bion attended to the existential conflict regarding tolerating emotional thinking, and how this conflict plays out in one's relationship to oneself and others, and within groups. Bringing a relational meaning to thinking, Bion emphasized its function of establishing emotional awareness of self and others. Recent writers have referred to this process as "mentalization" (Fonagy and Target, 1998).

"Thinking" involves establishing a "mental relationship with a personality—and of that personality's emotional experience—either the individual's own or that of another person" (Bion, 1962, p. 53).

> On a short international flight of one hour, my wife and I found ourselves behind a young mother and her seven month-old girl. The baby turned to us, staring into one set of eyes, and then the other, until we prepared for landing. Her wide-eyed scrutinizing compelled our full attention, and we put aside our reading to smile and make sounds and hand gestures. Secure in physical embrace of her mother, she sought to make sense of other human beings, and therefore, of herself. We felt drawn to mentalize with her in the motoric-paraverbal dialect we could share.

Bion hypothesized that every individual had the potential to develop a *psychoanalytic function of the personality* that utilizes this type of thinking. Without recourse to Bion's formulation, Pichon-Rivière (2017, p. 80) described how the mentalizing function develops in treatment: "When analysands leave the session, they start an introspective movement; they internalize their analyst and begin an internal dialogue with him. An internal link is established that last far beyond the hour of clinical analysis and provides a space for the development of self-analysis."

In group, internal links are established among all participants and contribute to the group's cohesion and coherence. However, when feeling insecure, the members tend to band together with thought-evading defenses, which Bion (1961) termed "*basic assumptions*" (*Chapter 4*). To advance the mentalizing process, we attempt to interest participation in the *workgroup*, in which members develop and utilize the self-analytical *psychoanalytic function of the personality*.

> A five-year member welcomed a confused newcomer with his own trajectory of "psychoanalytic education:" "They all had that psych lingo that I didn't get. How would that help with my problems? It took me a couple of years to understand what they were talking about and to begin doing it."

To "do it" requires us also to focus on the truths of our own experiences as leader. For, "the only justification for our concepts and system of concepts is that they serve to represent the complex of our experiences; beyond this they have no legitimacy" (Einstein, 1922, p. 2). One great lesson of 20th-century physics is that there is no absolute frame of reference. We have our experience of the experience of group members, and they have their experience of us. If we speak as well as listen, it is more likely that each session will direct itself toward the "psychoanalytic function."

About my Perspective

Bion imparted a mode of clinical thinking: to evaluate communications, my own as well as others', in terms of their use or purpose in establishing, questioning, investigating, challenging, or obstructing meaning. Through this lens I have developed concepts – as well as a praxis – reflected in what follows.

I integrate Freudian and Kleinian core concepts, Bion's early group theory (1961) and his later metapsychology regarding emotional meaning (1962; 1963; 1965; 1970), and contemporary psychoanalytic and group thinking. I incorporate the contributions of the French school (Lacan, Laplanche, and Kaës), the Argentinians Racker (1968), Pichon-Rivière (2017), and the

Barangers (2008), and my own work (Billow, 2003; 2010a; 2015; 2021a; 2021b; 2024). The goals here are those I pursue in my groups: to invite a relationship with the reader and to activate mental links at varying levels of development. Although I lean on Bion's object relations theory of thinking, his metapsychological formulations tend to mystify and obscure their broad clinical utility. I will present terms that more closely approximate my own group experiences as leader, member, and observer.

My approach is emotionally focused and yet cognitive, concerned with the interplay of *nuclear ideas*, consolidating concepts that bring depth and complexity to the group situation and to the mind of each individual. Ideas are never just "cogitations," but are attached to people who embody and carry them. As a member's ideas develop and change via immersion in the group, the relationships to these inner and outer objects change as well, as does behavior. *The ideas that we as analysts bring, develop, and offer shape and organize our groups.*

Bion tended to exalt the analyst as the "seer" or "exceptional individual." In the communal space of group, the analyst-leader is not the sole arbiter of psychoanalytic truth and may not be as effective as other members in reaching it. No one is exempt from the conflict between thinking and avoiding pain and all of us may detour, delay, and obstruct learning from experience. Hence, the *3Rs: resistance, rebellion*, and *refusal* (*Chapter 6*). It is preferable to speak in down-to-earth vernacular, convey compassion, and avoid sounding omniscient or oracular.

Previously-published works offer fuller accounts and detailed clinical examples, which hopefully make my formulations – and interventions based on them – compelling and experience-near. Yet I recognize some irony; although I am skeptical of psychological self-reports and narratives (common in groups), and of their veracity (other than mythic), I have written a lot of them (Billow, 2003; 2010; 2015; 2021a; 2021b; 2024a; 2024b). Bion (1975, p. 185) spoke to this issue in evaluating presentations by other analysts: "you are not obliged to say whether you regard the scientific papers as works of fiction or not. But you can form some opinion of the kind of fiction that those particular analysts write, or the kind of reality which they describe."

I suggest that all theories, formulations, and case presentations are in some ways retrofitted or aligned to the personality of the formulizer. Group praxis involves an admixture of a deductive approach, based on allegiances to particular theories and techniques, and an inductive approach based on observed experience and co-participation (Horwitz, 1977). Technique flows from theory, and in the other direction too, and both one's theories and techniques need to be "well suited" to the therapist (Freud, 1912). For, in deciding what aspects of clinical interactions should be dealt with, and in what terms, "to a great extent the choice is already determined by the analyst's personality" (Bion 1965, p. 166).

Therapists of all persuasions bring assumptions and foundational concepts to clinical work. We enter our offices carrying deeply-rooted identifications, perspectives, and reality beliefs based on our early development in a family and a particular culture. Issues of power, status, gender, race, age, and current social norms also inform and structure our thinking and behavior. Our mindsets, as flexible as we may believe them to be, lead to certain paths and foreclose others. Ideally, we allow ourselves unexplored places, stimulated by the thinking and writings of our clinical colleagues and prodded by those we work with.

Chapter 2

How is Group Psychotherapy Psychoanalytic?

To orient the reader, I present contrasting attitudes of Freud and Bion regarding groups and the view of institutional psychoanalysis toward group psychotherapy. I define specific qualities of a psychoanalytic group. Freud cautioned against isolating individual psychology and "neglecting all traces" of the group. For "the psychology of groups is the oldest human psychology; what we have isolated as individual psychology…has since come into prominence out of the old group psychology, by a gradual process which may still, perhaps, be described as incomplete" (Freud, 1921, p. 123). Yet Freud did not trust groups, emphasizing their irrationality and tendency toward regression. Focusing on mass and mob formations and on civilization itself, Freud (1921) characterized human beings as "horde animals" that seek and follow a leader to assure mutual protection against siblings and the leader as well.

Many have suggested that institutional psychoanalysis' characterization of groups and aversion to praxis may have been inaugurated by Freud himself, who acknowledged conflicts with siblings, peers, and groups (Agger, 1988; Benhaim, 2008; Campos Avilar, 1992; Rapheal-Leff, 1990). Freud was not a good group leader, recognizing his failure in establishing "friendly relations" among the cohorts (Jones, Rank, Abraham, and Ferenczi) of the Wednesday Evening Society technical seminar (in Jones, 1955). However, Freud did not study the individual in the therapy group or contemplate how a group approach may further therapeutic goals such that each member may benefit. Bion, the most prominent group theorist after Freud, attempted to do this, along with

DOI: 10.4324/9781032703251-3

his contemporary, S. H. Foulkes, and a few other pioneers such as Trigant Barrow, Norbert Elias, and Pichon-Rivière (see Ettin, 1999; Scharff, Losso, and Setton, 2017; Pertegato and Pertegato, 2013; Rutan, Stone, and Shay, 2014).

Bion (1961, p. 39) reflected Freud's emphasis on the group as stimulating an infantile desire to be led: "Either the desire for a leader is some emotional survival operating uselessly in the group as archaism, or else there is some awareness of a situation, which we have not defined, which demands the presence of such a person." However, contra to Freud, and speaking for many current practitioners, Bion (1961, p. 175) also maintained that "intellectual activity of a high order is possible in a group." He underscored that the very ability to think depends on "the social capacity of the individual. This development, of great importance in group dynamics, has received virtually no attention; its absence would make even scientific communication impossible" (Bion, 1962, p. 185). Bion (1962, p. 141) asserted that: "it can always be seen that some mental activity is directed to the solution of the problems for which the individuals seek help." Still, perhaps reflecting the intergenerational transmission of Freud's attitudes, Bion's analyst, Melanie Klein, dissuaded him from pursuing his ground-breaking therapeutic work, and he returned to the subject of the group only in his final volume of metapsychological writings (Bion, 1970).

In a critique of psychoanalytic education, Kernberg (2000) recognized the striking avoidance of studying the essential literature of small and large groups. He did not, however, go so far as to suggest structured and ongoing group experience among his proposals to address what he diagnosed as authoritarian pathology in these oligarchic and parochial training organizations. Perhaps encouraging is that in 2020, members of the *American Psychoanalytic Association* organized leader-led support groups to meet the crisis of COVID-19 and informal self-study groups remain prevalent today.

Shared Assumptions of Psychodynamic Group Psychotherapies

From one point of view, all group psychodynamic group therapies dwell within the broad church of Freud, a major cultural figure of the 20th century, which some have called the "Freudian century." Following Freud, we rely on "talk therapy" in the treatment of mental dysfunction, including trauma, neurosis, "borderline" and other characterological syndromes, and psychosis. Psychodynamic group therapists of all persuasions evaluate individuals by their patterns of thinking, affect, and behavior, and attend to the quality of the therapeutic relationship. We think of group process and here-and-now social realities. We look for individual patterns, group themes, and latent meanings. Countertransference, more broadly defined as co-participation, is no longer considered primarily as an obstacle remediated by treatment and self-study, but as an opportune therapeutic instrument. Concepts of "introjection–projection," "empathic immersion," "intersubjectivity," "implicit relational knowing," "co-construction," "analytic field," and "thirdness" are contemporary refinements of the old-fashioned, but still pertinent, idea of "clinical intuition." Still, "clinical touch" cannot be defined, and two group leaders may think alike and make similar interventions at similar moments with quite different results.

Despite similarities and convergences, organizational group therapy, like that of the church and traditional psychoanalysis, has been marked by rebellion and sectarianism. Schisms lead to creative, break-away groups; and yet the new institutions, like the old, tend to be organized hierarchically around iconic figures, and enforce allegiance with the threat or actuality of excommunication. A metaphoric ocean exists between the prominent American schools that are dominated by a here-and-now interpersonal approach, and English, European, and Latin American schools that integrate different amalgams of Freudian–Kleinian–Winnicottean-Bionian theory focusing on group-as-whole and unconscious processes on both individual and group levels. The history of *the International Association for Group Psychotherapy and Group Process* (*IAGP*) bears fierce splits and rivalries between "group therapists" and "psychodramatists;" an uneasy truce exists between the two.

Psychotherapy is under continual pressure to move toward a behavioral or psychopharmacological approach, emphasizing short-term treatment that is narrowly focused on symptom reduction. Concurrently, psychoanalytically-informed approaches are experiencing a renaissance, with new journals and podcasts broadening the scope of our work. Post-Freudian psychoanalytic thinking and writing adds currency and complexity to psychodynamic group formulations. In contrast, concepts derived from group psychotherapy have had little impact on psychoanalysis proper. Perhaps reflecting my bias, a question persists whether a clear and comprehensive theory of group exists, or could exist, cut off from the nourishing roots of psychoanalysis.

Prominent theorists such as Moreno and Pichon-Rivière did little writing themselves and depended on their students to convey their ideas, and certain group texts (such as Kaës, Bion [1970] and for Americans, Foulkes) are difficult to comprehend and integrate into the group literature. Regarding the founder of *Group Analysis*, his admiring colleague, Skynner (1983), acknowledged that conceptualization was not one of Foulkes' strong points, and the attraction was to him and therefore to his ideas. The textbooks and practitioners of psychodynamic group therapy tend to be eclectic and take their inspiration from their own integration of group dynamic, psychoanalytic, and interpersonal theories. Pines and Marrone (1990) spoke for many ideological group approaches – perhaps for all – when they wrote that while *Group Analysis* has a theoretical and methodological identity, it integrates different perspectives; most are psychoanalytic.

Psychoanalytic group psychotherapy is not psychoanalysis as defined by what Gill (1994) described as its extrinsic features – such as the dyadic setting, session frequency, use of the couch, and so forth – but it is psychoanalytic, given that "the wide scope of the current forms of psychoanalytic therapy allows room for many ideas, which do not even have to be restricted to the field of psychoanalysis in the stricter sense" (Thoma and Kachele, 1994, p. 188).

Freud (1914, p. 16). described two intrinsic qualities of psychoanalysis that extend to the psychoanalytic group: transference and resistance. "Any line of investigation which recognizes these two facts and takes them as the starting-point of its work has a right to call itself psycho-analysis." Freud (1923, p. 247) later expanded the principal subject matters of psychoanalysis to include "unconscious mental processes, the recognition of the theory of resistance and repression, the appreciation of the importance of sexuality and of the Oedipus Complex." Bion (1965, pp. 49–50) put it thus: "Freud stated as one of the criteria by which a psychoanalyst was to be judged was the degree of understanding allegiance he paid to the theory of the Oedipus complex...and time has done nothing to suggest that he erred by overestimation; evidence of the Oedipus complex is never absent though it can be unobserved." Pichon-Rivière (2017, p. 91) emphasized that the psychoanalytic approach entails "the systematic search for the third part and an inquiry into the role it is playing in the here-and-now with us. We should always keep in mind that thinking, loving, and hating never take place in a two-person relationship; we are always dealing with three people."

Every social group is characterized by triangular relationships involving three protagonists: the member, the leader, and the group itself (Garland, 2010). Other threesomes emerge from this rubric. The psychoanalytic therapist brings an Oedipal perspective to whatever emerges in the group's discourse and enactments. To do that, however, the therapist needs to be equipped with a deep understanding of developmental and unconscious roots of character and behavior – *learned from the inside*. "Analysts must be aware that they are also analyzing themselves and that they are using tools, internal objects and fantasies, that are their own and not others" (Pichon-Rivière, 2017, p. 92). Garland (2010, p. 10) cautioned that poorly analyzed and trained therapists run groups that risk becoming "psychological health farm[s] promoting an internationally accredited diet of altruism, universality, acceptance, self-disclosure," and so forth. Developing a sophisticated "group self," members build "a carapace of revised social skills." To hone potential therapeutic talents, in-depth psychoanalytic and group psychoanalytic education, personal and group analysis, and supervision are essential.

Chapter 3

Genealogy

Chapter 3 considers the recent history of the group therapy movement, key differences among psychoanalytically inspired psychodynamic modes, and the overlaps that exist in actual practice. Helen Durkin (1964) identified three models, derived from three ideological orientations: *traditional psychoanalytic, interpersonal*, and *group dynamic (group as a whole)*. Each was inspired by a psychoanalytically-informed, charismatic figure or figures possessing the energy and enthusiasm to generate audiences and adherents, and establish organizations, journals, and texts. These are historic and foundational categories, which I reclassify according to subsequent developments in group theory and practice.

Psychoanalytic Models

Classical and Contemporary

The Freudian psychoanalytic model, modified to address the circumstances of group psychotherapy, directed the formation and early years of the *American Group Psychological Association* and had wide influence (Slavson, 1964; Wolf and Schwarz, 1962). Slavson (1957, p. 181) advised the analytic therapist to "nip in the bud" group dynamics in order to concentrate on the individual. "Group cohesion has to be prevented so that each can communicate his problems and work them through." However, group dynamics cannot be nipped; rather, the analytically oriented

DOI: 10.4324/9781032703251-4

therapist attempts to understand the components of a group's process and culture and integrate them in our interventions. While giving time for individual exploration is an essential feature, psychoanalytic group therapy is not individual psychoanalysis in the group. Other members do not sit passively, but join, offering their own relevant experiences and making helpful clarifications and on-point interpretations. *Relational group psychotherapy* extends the principal subject matter to include the analyst's subjectivity and the "analytic field" in which all participants participate.

Different psychoanalytic persuasions vary in the leader's use of the "analyzing instrument," through which psychoanalytic interventions are offered (Isakower, 1992; Jacobs, 1992). Closer to the classical tradition are analytically oriented therapists who adhere to the dictum "put it into words." They are apt to offer interpretative hypotheses linking developmental conflicts and traumas to the individual and group's defences, fantasies, and symbolic themes, related to transference phenomena centering around the therapist (*vertical* transferences) and sibling relationships (*horizontal* transferences). *Group Analytic* (Foulksian), *interpersonal*, and *self-psychological* group therapists tend to be conservative in making interpretations, seeing their function as securing a firm base for the members to share in the "intermediate territory" of play (Winnicott, 1971) and find their own voices. Influenced by the studies on post-traumatic disorders (PTSD), some analysts organize the group around "witnessing," or "being with" (Grossmark, 2007; Reis, 2009), in which the therapist's "unobtrusive" presence facilitates recovery and growth.

Group Analytic (Foulkesian)

Originating in England and prominent in Europe, Israel, and Latin America, the *Group Analytic* model shares features of both a *psychoanalytic* and a *group dynamic* model. Its founder, S.H. Foulkes, and early adherents were psychoanalysts and integrated psychoanalytic formulations, as do many of its prominent contemporary contributors, such as Pines and Hopper. However, Foulkes also was influenced by Kurt Goldstein's gestalt-informed, neurological perspective and Norbert Elias' (1939/2000) view of group participants as forming a "configuration," or points of connection, and that they should be analyzed as a unit (Barwick and Weegmann, 2018). Foulkes used *"psychic matrix"* as the metaphor for nurturing and growth. ("Matrix" derives from the Latin word meaning mother.) The individual and group exist as figure-ground phenomena, and within this "hypothetical web of communication and relationship" each member exists as a "nodal point" (Foulkes, 1964, p. 292). Three "locations," foci of group interactions, are prominent: the *personal matrix*, referring to the workings of the individual mind; the *dynamic matrix*, referring to interpersonal processes; and the *foundation matrix*, referring to biological properties and the culturally-embedded values and reactions that underlie therapeutic and social groups (Powell, 1994). Hopper (2003) utilized the concept of the *foundation matrix* in his formulation of the *"social unconscious."*

The fulcrum of analytic work involves free floating group discussion, equivalent to the free-association process of dyadic psychoanalysis. A maturing, healing process occurs as members shift from *monologues* (self-centered) to *dialogical* (interpersonal) interactions, and finally, to group-embracing *discourse* (Schlapobersky, 2016). In the process of becoming a contributing group member, the individual's self-centered, neurotic tendencies gradually dissipate. The group conductor engages in withdrawal and decentralization such that the group, freed from compliance and self-subjugation to the leader, comes to do the work (Barwick and Weegmann, 2018, p. 28).

However, Hopper, a member of one of Foulkes' groups, reported that Foulkes maintained an active presence and interpreted on both group and individual levels (personal communication, 2023). Having participated in and observed groups led by Pines and Hopper, I found both leaders to be magnetic forces. Pines' group-centered interventions tended to be soothing and brought members together, while Hopper's interventions, directed to individuals as well as to the group, are rarely restful, often challenging, and sometimes confronting.

The prominent individuals who identify as group analysts have gone in interesting directions, integrating other psychoanalytic and sociological perspectives. As the heir apparent of Foulkes, Pines incorporated Winnicott and self-psychology (Harwood and Pines, 1998). As mentioned above, Hopper (2003) designated a determinative "social unconscious" that impacts the psychology of the person, interpersonal relations, and culture. Extending Bion's group formulations, Hopper (1997) proposed a fourth *basic assumption*, which he identified as *Incohesion: Aggregation/ Massification* (I:AM). When preoccupied with *annihilation anxieties*, groups do not really cohere; rather, they form fragmented *aggregates* of isolated individuals, or alternatively, *mass* and fuse together via a shared illusion of solidarity.

Developing a theory and practice of the *Large Group*, Kreeger (1975) brought together contributions from Foulkes, Pines, Hopper, and others. Composed of 30 or more participants with several leaders, *Large Group* experiences are designed to advance "outsight" (social insight): "the outward expansion of social consciousness and thoughtfulness" (de Mare, 1997). *Large Group* experiences have been included in the introductory group work course of the *Institute of Group Analysis* since the late 1960s; they are a popular feature of AGPA annual conferences, led by leaders of different theoretical orientations (Schneider and Weinberg, 2003).

Another offshoot of Group Analysis is the *Social Dreaming Group*, pioneered by Gordon Lawrence and his colleagues at the Tavistock Institute in the 1980s. The *dynamic matrix* of *social dreaming* captures aspects of unconscious processes and interpersonal dynamics present but unattended to in social relationships. The social dreaming technique focusses on the dream, the associational interconnections among members, and emergent meaning, not on the dreamer (Friedman, 2019; Long and Manley, 2019). The *Social Dreaming International Network* (SDIN) was established in 2019.

Self-psychological and Intersubjective

Breaking away from Freud's (1914) concept of narcissism as a developmental failure and a source of pathology, Heinz Kohut developed a theory in which the development of healthy narcissism was the achievement of a creative, cohesive self, and hence, the goal of treatment. He conceived of the self as an innate structure that regulates self-esteem (narcissism), and which follows a different developmental line from the Oedipal trajectory of object love (Newirth, 2023, p. 50). Although Kohut wrote of a "group self" with specific "selfobject" (developmental) needs parallel to the individual, he did not approve of group therapy, distrusting a charismatic leader's potential use of power (Arensberg, 1990). However, he served as the pivotal transitional figure in the development of the *self-psychological group approach*, a central tenet being that self-experience is shaped by an "intersubjective" context in which it crystallizes.

Kohut described three types of "selfobject" needs that lead to the formation of transferences and the roles that the therapist must fulfil to address deficits in the development of healthy narcissism: *mirroring, idealization*, and forming a *twinship*. In *mirroring*, the group therapist supports expressions of grandiosity, aggression, and sexuality. Embracing the member and group's *idealizations*, the therapist responds to needs for energetic, strong, and soothing leadership. *Twinship* communication conveys "we-ness," that the therapist shares the values, ideas, and attitudes of other participants. "*Transmuting internalizations*" occur as members experience empathic failures, trace their unconscious roots in personal history, and restore trust in therapeutic relationships. Kohut made no references to Winnicott, who earlier had formulated concepts regarding "good enough" mothering (and fathering) (Mitchell and Black, 1996). The *self-psycholgical/intersubjective model* emphasizes the importance of the therapist's emotional availability and warmth. Understanding provided by empathic immersion allows for the subsequent explanatory bringing together of the dynamic and genetic underpinnings of the patient's subjective experience (Stolorow, Magid, Fosshage, and Shane, 2021).

Sullivanian Interpersonal (Yalom)

The six editions of Yalom's (1995; Yalom and Leszcz, 2020) *The Theory and Practice of Group Psychotherapy* have served as guidebooks for the *interpersonal model*, utilized internationally in ambulatory, impatient, and day hospital settings, and across a range of diagnoses. Yalom's approach is rooted in the theories of Harry Stack Sullivan (1953), who proposed that the basic motives guiding human behavior are achieving interpersonal attachment and reducing anxiety. Psychological disorder reflects disturbance that originated in the misattunement of caregivers. In efforts at self-care, the confused and isolated child develops a rigid character structure and a system of "*selective inattention*" to feedback that would disconfirm the "*parataxic distortions*" (pathogenic perceptions and beliefs) that accrue over time.

Also integrating a wide selection of contemporary psychodynamic theories and research, Yalom's model of interpersonal group psychotherapy centers upon the mutative role of interpersonal interaction, feedback, and learning. The group mirrors the individual's relational world in a here-and-now context. Maladaptive interpersonal patterns of behavior, distorted core beliefs, and misconstruals of the intentions and actions of others become reactivated. Effective group treatment offers a corrective emotional experience. Pathological cognitive interpersonal schemas (Weiss et al., 1986) are disconfirmed in the supportive context of new relational experiences. While increasing self-awareness (insight) may be useful for some individuals, genetic reconstructions are not essential to the curative processes.

Yalom and Leszcz (2020) list specific therapeutic factors, including: altruism, mutual support, cohesion, the sense of belonging to the group, feeling understood and accepted, universality, guidance, helpful and accurate information, catharsis, self-understanding, and the instillation of hope. (See research findings in Macnair-Semands, Ogrodniczuck, and Joyce, 2010.) Interventions are conveyed in an atmosphere of positive regard. Although Yalom and Leszcz advised the therapist to gradually step back and trust the group to do the work, Yalom (1995) remained an active leadership presence, going so far as to send members detailed post-session summaries.

Modern Group Analytical

Modern Group Analysis developed from the theories of Hyman Spotnitz, guided by Freud's (1940) statement that "all of psychoanalysis has to be reformulated in terms of understanding the aggressive drive as separate from the libidinal drive" (in Spotnitz and Meadow, 1976, p. 4). For Spotnitz, the primary determinant of psychopathology involved an organizing, pre-Oedipal "narcissistic defense," characterized by self-hate rather than self-love, and which directed aggression inward to protect primary objects.

> The more the patient feels his aggressive impulses and expresses them in words charged with genuine emotion, the more aware he becomes of his love impulses and the easier it is for him to act on them unobstructively in healthful and socially constructive ways.
> (Spotnitz and Meadow, 1976, p. 30)

Given that most mental disturbances originate before language development, transferences are most often expressed through behavior, symptoms, and symbolic communications. Of primary importance are transmissions of the patient's feeling states, which induce the analyst's potentially informative "*objective countertransferences.*"

Spotnitz advised to initially "join" the patient's resistance and allow the verbal expression of aggression without challenge. In time, however, the therapist has to help the patient develop new patterns for impulse control and regulation. Spotnitz was alert to the danger of a sympathetic, soothing approach, which would entrench the patient's customary defences that guard against the release of hostility (Spotnitz and Meadow, 1976, p. 41). He was also one of the first psychoanalysts to advocate the use of groups.

Spotnitz' theories and techniques were furthered by Louis Ormont (1992), who put forth a systematic method of enhancing "*emotional communication*" and identifications among members. Ormont developed the technique of "*bridging*," encouraging group participants to join, resonate with, or opine regarding another's member's presentation. He mandated a "group contract" to put all thoughts and feelings in words. However, it is a contract designed to be contested or even broken. Given their neurotic and characterological difficulties, and engrossed in the intensity of the group, members are often uncooperative and noncompliant, and resistant to Oedipal level communication. Resistances convey the members' current difficulties in living and provide the opportunity for individuals to observe themselves and others and modify their behaviors (Zeisel, 2012).

As with so many group theorists, Ormont claimed that his techniques placed the group, rather than the leader, as center of the action. Having been a member in several of Ormont's training groups, I found a skilful leader taking full advantage of a showbusiness background. A witty master of ceremonies, Ormont kept the action going with quick shifts from member to member, adjusting the emotional temperature in the room by uncovering unexpressed feelings, or provoking them, stressing the affective dimensions (rather than the intellectual content) of communications, and intermittently interpreting transferences. Most *Modern analysts* work at a more measured pace and make less use of a humorously ironic presence. While still relying on the bridging technique, they offer and give more space for reflection and empathic resonance (e.g., Levine, 2011).

In 1975, Spotnitz inspired the formation of the *Center for Modern Psychoanalytic Studies* (*CMPS*), an analytic training institute and journal, *Modern Psychoanalysis. The Center for Group Studies* (*CGS*), founded in 1989, has emerged as an international training institution, designed around Ormont's principles and techniques.

The French Psychoanalytic Model: Lacan, Laplanche, and Kaës

The early Freudian topographical model of the mental apparatus (the three mental systems of unconscious, preconscious, and conscious), the prominent role of infantile sexuality, and the importance of dream and linguistic analysis remain alive in French psychoanalysis. Lacan, Laplanche, Kaës, the three authors I refer to specifically, rescue relational psychoanalysis from an excessive here-and-now, interactive focus. (Only Kaës specifically focuses on the group.) They resurrect concepts of inborn structure, instincts (or constitutional drives), the inescapable traumas of birth, separation, and the realization of "otherness" (alterity). Transference interpretations, which are frequent, often bypass defences to delve into unconscious conflicts, "phantasies" (unconscious fantasies), and desires that center around archaic sexuality and aggression.

Lacan remains the towering figure. While he was not a group analyst, Lacan was strongly influenced by the early work of Bion, which he characterized as marking "a historic date in psychiatry" (Lacan, 1947, in Giraldo, 2012, p. xv). From a Lacan lens, the group reflects the *Real* of drive and trauma, the *Imaginary* of attachment and seduction, and the *Symbolic* of language. The *Imaginary* order is foremost; it is the region in which inner infantile objects and phantasies activate and create the narratives and enactments of the group. Lacan also revived Freud's early concept of *nachtraglichkeit*, the retroactive reconstruction of early experience, which has emerged as the "essence" of a contemporary psychoanalytic approach (Birksted-Breen, 2016, p. 21; see *Chapter 3*).

Laplanche, Lacan's former student and analysand, adopted Althusser's (1971) concept of "interpellation," the cultural implantation of implicit messages, proclaiming "revolutionary" his "decentered" psychoanalytic theory. Returning to Freud's original (but later rejected) seduction theory, Laplanche (1992) proposed that the infant is "immediately and completely immersed" in "enigmatic messages," some never to be adequately understood. Enigmatic messages are transmitted without awareness by nurturing figures who themselves have been similarly implanted. Apropos are Freud's (1905, p. 223) remarks: "A mother would probably be horrified if she were made aware that all her marks of caring (derived from her own sexual life) were rousing her child's sexual instinct and preparing for its later intensity...She is only fulfilling her task in teaching the child to love." The Laplanchian self is never fully present in here-and-now *interpersonal* life; an *intrasubjective* self remains preoccupied with the enigma of its existence, blindly coping with compelling messages, many of an unrealized sexualized and aggressive nature.

Availing himself of Klein's seminal "inner world" concept of internalized objects and part-objects, Kaës (2007) proposed that dynamic "*internal groups*" formed the basis of unconscious mental life. *Internal groups* do not originate exclusively from interiorizations of psychosocial relationships, but from an inborn "groupality," a mental predisposition to symbolize and form intersubjective "links." Family members and relationships come to serve as prototypes and, in the course of development, other individuals acquire symbolic functions as mothers, fathers, sisters, and brothers. In the *actual group*, members come to personify these figures and relationships and the unconscious "messages" that were conveyed. The group serves as a vehicle for (partial) translations in which the therapist's consistent interpretations of pre-Oedipal, sibling, and Oedipal phantasies reoccurring in ongoing group relationships serve as the curative "metapsychic" that transforms the participants (see *Chapters 4 and 5*).

Operative Groups (Pichon-Rivière)

Pichon-Rivière's work, fundamental to Latin American psychoanalytic development, is largely unknown in English-language psychoanalysis and group psychotherapy (Scharff, Losso, and Setton, 2017). Pichon-Rivière (1907–1977) hypothesized a proto depression occurring at birth as the infant separates from the mother's womb. To protect against total helplessness, the infant forms a "*vínculo*" (an interactive link) with the mother. "Links" to other key developmental figures follow, such that the mind becomes structured as a group. As with Kaës (2017), who independently developed his own strikingly-similar concepts, Pichon-Rivière asserted that links have two axes, *vertical* and *horizontal.* In the *vertical axis*, the subject is tied in transgenerational *vínculos* to parents, ancestors, and authorities. In the *horizontal axis*, the subject is linked to contemporaries such as partners and the community and culture of peers (Scharff, Losso, and Setton, 2017).

Pichon-Rivière (2017) characterized psychopathology as a stereotyped structure resembling a vicious closed circle, analogous to Freud's description of libidinal fixation. Excessive defensive formations lead to *disposition points*, wherein the "*spiral*" of communication and mutual learning stagnates; the dialectic interplay with the environment becomes *inoperative. Disposition points* happen at various stages in a person's development and remain latent in the unconscious until retriggered by current conflict, the *emergent* (emergency point). The analyst's task is to establish or re-establish a *spiral* process to break or open the rigid closed structures (referred to by the Barangers as *bastions*) that entrap the analysand in a repetitive cycle of psychopathology (Romero-Garcia, 2021, p. 77).

Resulting from the analyst's successful interpretations of the *emergent's* links to repressed or dissociated past situations, a new *existent* (thesis) occurs. Thus, insight restarts the thesis–antithesis–synthesis of the *spiral* learning process (Tubert-Oklander and Hernández de Tubert, 2004). In treatment following the *operative group model*, the group therapist's interventions are directed to help members discover the past links to their *emergents*, integrate their split roles, and develop insight into the *stereotypical* roles they assign and assume in interpersonal relationships.

Greenberg (2018) credited Pichon-Rivière as among the most important contributors to psychoanalysis through his influence on generations of colleagues and students, most prominently, the Barangers. Their (Baranger, et. al., 1983) concept of the "*analytic field*" enlarged the analytic paradigm from a two-person interaction to a two-person group, both participating in a psychic entity (the relationship), a "third" that structures the participation of both parties. Brown (2017, p. 268) saw a parallel concept in Bion's *basic assumptions*, referring to the pool of shared unconscious phantasies that to some degree determined each member's experience. However, for Bion, it was essential for the therapist to step *out* of the pool, while for Pichon-Rivière and the Barangers, the analyst remains immersed in it. "Analysts' every movement and behavior affect patients' unconscious and produces modification in the field that, in turn, act upon analysts themselves" (Pichon-Rivière, 2017, p. 79). Pichon-Rivière worked closely with Heinrich Racker, who also emphasized the unconscious dimensions of mutual influence, although Pichon-Rivière did not share Racker's insistent focus on the analyst's (infantile) subjectivity and vulnerability to countertransference enactment. Like Kaës, Pichon-Rivière emphasized the importance of the therapist's explication of transference in relationship to the members' *internal groups* and unconscious early desires and phantasies, but without a full consideration of his own inevitable transferences. I have offered a therapist-inclusive, relational counterpoint (Billow, 2024a).

Group Dynamic Models

Group dynamic models focus primarily on the psychodynamics of the whole group, its process, themes, fantasies, and defences. The group functions as a superindividual, subject to therapeutic regression and disarray. The overriding assumption is that people will learn about themselves through the study of how they function in groups and relate to other members and the leader(s). Via the group process, members come to locate and free themselves from controlling intrapsychic and interpersonal sources, both historic and current. While Lewin and Bion (along with Freud) are guiding figures, neither authored a model geared for clinical settings.

Kurt Lewin and T-Groups

Although psychodynamic theories describing organizational life appeared as early as 1911 (Wren and Greenwood, 1998), Kurt Lewin (1890–1947) is considered the father of social psychology and group dynamics (the latter, a term he originated). Influenced by Gestalt psychology and a background in psychoanalysis, Lewin proposed a "*Field Theory.*" To understand the individual, the whole psychological field of its "*lifespace*" had to be considered. Remediation of psychological disturbance occurs when individuals forgo pure egocentricism and relate as parts of a whole; that is, as members of a group. Lewin described group dynamics as involving four components: *driving forces, restraining forces, forces for change*, and the *forces resisting change*. Each force has its own impact on decisions regarding whether to preserve an egocentric (or collective) *status quo* or push for positive change.

Introduced to the concept of "encounter" by his early mentor, Jacob Moreno (who later developed *Psychodrama*), Lewin first conceived of experiential learning as a research technique, yet his theories regarding group-centered dynamics have become foundational. *Training groups (T-groups)* and *Encounter Groups* emerged in the 1960s as "*humanistic*" modalities promoting individual growth. The journal *Human Relations* addresses personal and social relationships, organizations, and wider political and economic systems. Working independently, Carl Rogers at the University of Chicago contributed to the interrelated "*sensitivity group*" movement.

Bion and Tavistock Human Relations Groups

The Tavistock or Human Relations Groups have their roots in the principles Bion (1961) established in his early papers on group. While influenced by Kurt Lewin's research on group dynamics, Bion's formulations derived from a group application of Melanie Klein's alteration of the primary–secondary process distinction. Klein had elaborated an ongoing interaction between two "*basic positions*" of the personality: "psychotic" and "neurotic/normal." The *psychotic* level, not necessarily clinically psychotic but dominated by primary processes, takes two forms, *paranoid-schizoid* and *depressive*. "*Psychotic*" anxieties underlie and are apt to enter into the neurotic-normal of everyday life.

Following Klein's psychotic/normal distinction, Bion (1961, p. 159) delineated "two different categories of mental activity [that] co-exist" in actual groups. Two types of thinking are implicated: a tripartite *basic assumption mentality* and a *workgroup mentality*. Three *basic assumptions* map onto Klein's *psychotic positions*. F/F (fight/flight) reflects the *paranoid-schizoid* position in which others are experienced as potentially dangerous. D (dependency) reflects the unresolved *depressive* position, in which members are preoccupied with receiving oral supplies (i.e., nurturance and love). P (pairing) represents what Klein referred to as a reactive "*manic defense*" posed to guard against emerging "*psychotic*" anxieties. *Pairing* occurs, for example, when group members become preoccupied with the messianic task of "curing" an individual or solving an individual's problems, ignoring their own psychologies. The *workgroup* is analogous to the *neurotic/normal* part of the personality that values logic, verbal formulation, and insight. In productive groups, under the auspices of its leader, *basic assumptions* and *workgroup* processes interact, each vitalizing and supplying information to the other (*Chapter 4*).

While Bion's (1961) early ideas have been integrated into our thinking about groups, interventions centering on *basic assumptions* defences and phantasies have not proved to be clinically effective. However, they structure the operation of "*Tavistock*" or *Human Relations Groups*, designed with the heuristic purpose of studying the relationship of the individual to organizations and to authority. Meetings are organized around experientially-intense, weekend or longer "conferences." The "consultants" or "facilitators" (leaders) monitor group process from a Bionic position of emotional distance and offer sparse, whole-group interpretations, both of which frustrate and potentiate regression often left unresolved at the conference's conclusion. Many attendees find the meetings stimulating and personally valuable and join a cadre of returnees. The Tavistock journal, *Human Relations*, was founded (in 1947) with two early papers by Lewin. The *A.K. Rice Institute* (*AKRI*), an offshoot, was imported to the United States in 1969 by Margaret Rioch. A. K. Rice, the Institute's namesake, had worked with the Tavistock Institute in London. A. K. Rice conferences are designed similarly to Tavistock's: to study the behavioral dynamics of small groups and larger social systems.

Agazarian's Systems-centered Approach

Yvonne Agazarian (1997) developed a "*living human systems theory*," drawing from an amalgam of psychoanalysis, systems and communication theory, and Lewin and Bion. *System-centered Therapy* (SCT), in contrast to the two approaches described above, was specifically designed for group psychotherapy. Agazarian defined a hierarchy of group subsystems: *person systems* provide the source of energy; *member systems* organize and form transient *subgroup systems*; and the *group system* integrates its subgroups. The systems are progressive and reversible, influencing and being influenced by each other.

Agazarian's approach differs from other group therapies in that the leader purposefully shapes the norms of communication rather than letting group processes develop. Following Lewinian precepts of *driving* and *restraining* group forces, the *SCT* leader tracks and redirects the group, deciding when its "energy" is oriented away from its primary developmental goals. Agazarian usefully distinguished between *functional subgroups* (which serve to contain differences until they can be integrated within the group as a whole) and *stereotype subgroups* that are estranged or oppositional. The *SCT* therapist educates members to participate in *functional subgroupings* and to respect the differences among divergent subgroups. By signalling "anyone else," a member invites others who share similarities and emotional resonances. Using a "*fork in the road*" exploratory technique, the leader advises members to choose between explaining and blocking experience, or participating in the experience itself.

Three successive group developmental stages are assumed operative. In the first *authority phase*, members externalize and blame one's difficulties on external authority. A "barometric event" (Bennis and Sheppard, 1956) occurs in which the members test the leader's resilience in the face of challenge and rebellion. In the second *intimacy phase*, the group moves from *flight/fight* defenses and "*role locks*" with peers and the leader to discussing and working through anxieties, coming to relate without splitting and polarization. In the *work phase*, members develop the emotional maturity to shift perspectives, appreciate similarities and differences among individuals, and realize one's position in larger social systems. Agazarian fostered a *Systems Centered Training and Research Institute* that has continued since her death under the leadership of Susan Gantt.

Psychodrama

Psychodrama serves as one of the principal modes of group treatment in Europe and Latin America and is often utilized in conjunction with psychoanalytic treatment (e.g., Kaës, 2007; Anzieu, 1984). Practicing psychodramatists tend to think psychoanalytically, employ similar concepts, value insight, and emphasize the links between present relationships and traumatic experiences with early nurturing figures. However, although a Viennese contemporary of Freud and his circle, its founder, Jacob Moreno (1889–1974), rejected traditional psychoanalysis' focus on the individual and drives. Moreno (1952) held that conscious and unconscious states of mind are defined by the roles one has adopted historically and continue to play out (similar to Pichon-Rivière's emphasis). He conceived of four developmental stages of infancy: finding personal identity (*doubling*), recognizing oneself (*mirroring*), conforming (developing an *auxiliary ego*), and recognizing the subjectivity of other persons (*role-reversal*). Psychodramatic techniques are based on these developmental stages.

A session proceeds in three phases, *warm-up, sharing*, and *group discussion*, and may focus on a single individual, referred to as the "protagonist." In *doubling*, another member acts out the protagonist's emotions and behaviors; in *mirroring*, members reenact (imaginary/suppressed) scenes, events, and conversations; in *role-playing*, the protagonist portrays the figure of conflict; and in *role reversal*, another member plays the part of the protagonist, who then takes on the role of the antagonist, e.g., the child becomes the parent, or vice-versa (Cruz, Sales, Alves, and Moita, 2018).

Guided by the therapist, referred to as "director," the protagonist obtains insight and catharsis by reenacting and rescripting sources of distress in the immediacy and creative spontaneity of the session. Other group members benefit by making relevant connections and obtaining personal insights (Paredes, 2015). Moreno also developed a related approach to groups and larger organizations that he referred to as "*sociometry*," focused on social relationships, including ethnic and unconscious factors, hidden beliefs, forbidden agendas, and ideologies. He founded the *American Society of Group Psychotherapy and Psychodrama (ASGPP)* in 1942.

The Relational Turn

By the turn of the 21st century, few psychodynamic therapists would argue that they were not "relational." Greenberg and Mitchell's (1983) *Object Relations in Psychoanalytic Theory* captured an intellectual *zeitgeist* and was instrumental in inaugurating a "*relational turn*" in psychoanalytic thinking and nomenclature. The authors located two opposing models of psychoanalysis: a classically-defined Freudian model, in which relations are determined by the individual's needs to satisfy innate sexual and aggressive drives (and the defences against them), and a "relational" model, in which object-seeking and actual relationships are primary. Basing formulations on H. S. Sullivan's interpersonal theory, they offered a "relational-conflict" perspective. Patients enter projecting and recreating familiar, constricted relational patterns. The therapeutic process involves relinquishing those ties sufficiently to open new and richer interpersonal relations.

Rather than consigned to a neutral role of witness and interpreter, Greenberg and Mitchell depicted the analyst as a "*participant-observer*," adopting Sullivan's term. The authors challenged Freud's belief in "psychoanalytic purification," i.e., that countertransference could be resolved by the therapist's own treatment.

In a 1997 panel of the *American Psychoanalytic Association's Annual Meeting*, the chair declared, "in today's world countertransference is God, and Heinrich Racker is its prophet" (Kelly, 1997, p. 1253). The Argentinian Kleinian described the analyst as a conflicted individual – no freer of unconscious influence than anyone else, despite training and personal treatment. The therapist's "internal and external dependencies, anxieties, and pathological defences…[respond] to every event of the analytic situation" (Racker, 1968, p. 132). In not acknowledging and grappling with one's own emotionality, the therapist promulgates the "myth of the 'analyst without anxiety or anger'." Racker cautioned that the myth represented a "great danger," a remnant of the traumatogenic "patriarchal order," an expression of "social inequality in the analyst-analysand society…and the need for social reform."

A "sea change" has occurred in our understanding of the analyst's participation (Greenberg, 2018, p. 983). Group therapy is a logical extension and natural fit with this new egalitarian sensibility, given its emphasis on reducing patient–therapist asymmetry and fostering a collaborative process. Still, the therapist possesses special knowledge and technical skills and maintains a separate and uniquely powerful role.

Cognitive-developmental psychology has come to occupy a center stage, as relational interests have broadened from the psychology of conflict to include a psychology of attachment patterns and developmental deficits and arrests. *Infancy research* has supported Bowlby's (1988) theory of the biological basis of attachment, confirming that neonates enter the world with an array of conceptual skills oriented to survival and human affiliation (Karen, 2024). Microanalyses of videoed infant–mother interactions have revealed very early patterns of communication between the two participants and mutual influence (Beebe and Lachmann, 2020). A prolonged period of mutual "eye love" between mother and infant occurs, involving not only the visual sense but also touch, sound, and movement (exteroception–interoception). In this "dance," each partner enjoyably makes moment-by-moment adjustments in response to the other's shifts in behaviors (Beebe and Lachman, 2020). Given our increased understanding of nonverbal communication, group therapists are alert to the performative dimensions of mental life, such as facial expression, eye contact, body positioning, and gesture.

Developmentalists challenge Freudian and Kleinian conceptualizations of psychopathology based on the model of an irrationally-driven, hallucinatory infantile mind. They describe normal infants as less organized rather than "primitive." While remaining dependent on a supportive caretaking environment, the baby's mind becomes increasingly complex and integrated (Seligman, 2003). An adequately nurturing environment serves as the moderating center of emotional development. However, for many analysts, the Kleinian baby has not been thrown out with the bathwater of discarded theory. Her formulations regarding the ongoing influence of "part-object" (good breast/bad breast) internal relationships, psychotic-like phantasies, and infantile defences of splitting, projection, and idealization have currency.

Ideas derived from *Critical Theory* have roused a "political turn" in relational psychoanalysis. The writings of the *Frankfurt School of Critical Theory* in the 1920s and 1930s remain influential. Founding members included T. W. Adorno, Herbert Marcuse, and Erich Fromm; later generations followed (e.g., Derrida, Foucault, and Habermas). *Critical Theory* views social relations from a vantage point of Marxism and Hegelian philosophy along with ideas drawn from psychoanalysis, sociology, existentialism, and linguistics. It presupposes a societal-embedded definition of knowledge. Neither value-free nor without purpose, meaning is constructed and utilized to advance certain human interests over others, so as to establish power balances and group domination (Guess, 1981). The Italian Marxist theorist Antonio Gramsci described a pervasive "hegemony" of the ruling political class that disarms the unfranchised through propagandistic institutions of state, church, and mass media (Fonseca, 2016). *The International Journal of Critical Pedagogy* was established in 2008.

Sociologically- and politically-oriented psychoanalytic and feminist theorists such as Benjamin (1988), Butler (1993), and Layton (2020) concentrate on essential but previously ignored intersubjective factors of psychoanalysis, such as inherent power disparities, cultural and sexual diversity, social privilege, "whiteness," xenophobia, post-colonialism, environmental trauma, and political injustice. Writing in El Salvador before being assassinated in 1989, the Jesuit scholar Martin-Baro (1994) proposed a "liberation psychology" to forthrightly address the historical contexts, social conditions, and aspirations of the disenfranchised and oppressed (see also Bermudez, 2019; Caputo and Tomai, 2020; Lykes and Moane, 2009). The *AGPA* and other organizations in the United States and abroad are attempting to integrate theories of inequality and oppression into group practice.

Convergences in Contemporary Psychoanalytic Therapy

Many, perhaps most, psychoanalytic therapists have relinquished dogmatic allegiances to a particular theory and approach and have become more emotionally and intellectually available and democratic. Traditional oppositions have been reassessed, such as between transference and countertransference, unconsciousness and consciousness, accommodation and interpretation, and words and action. Theorists agree on the central role of relationships in the origin and maintenance of reflective thought. Their interests have broadened from the dynamics of the Oedipal period to earlier or "pre-Oedipal" triangular relationships, and to the earliest stages of development before language acquisition.

Common Denominators of Contemporary Psychoanalytic Group Approaches

1 Developing and maintaining positive therapeutic relationships, especially between each member and the group therapist (bonding and cohesion as primary curative vectors).
2 Focussing on the "here and now" of affective (emotional) experience.
3 Accommodating developmental "gaps" and needs.

4 Privileging insight into unconscious and dissociated individual and group experience (replacing the pejorative "acting out" with a normative concept of "enactment").
5 Giving weight to the "there and then" of trauma and early family development and its influences on the individual and group's "here and now" ("internal groups" vis a vis the actual group, *Chapter 4*).
6 Shifting from a concentration on *what* one thinks to *how* (Kohon and Perelberg, 2018; Ogden, 2011), which requires attending to nonverbal dimensions of experience and communication, and to alterations in availability of symbolic thinking ("mentalizing").
7 Attending to sibling relationships, symbolic, transferential, and actual (*Chapter 5*).
8 Attending to "socio-group dynamics," differences in culture, identity, privilege, and power, and how they factor into the "co-constructed" therapeutic experience.
9 Recognizing a "transsubjective" psychic reality: a "social unconscious" (Hopper, 2003) of interpellated socio-cultural ideas, transmitted intergenerationally (Laplanche, 1999).

Part II

Core Concepts

Chapter 4

The Expanded Psychoanalytic Group Frame

As with other treatment modalities, psychoanalytic group therapy has annexed new ideas and pluralistic views, expanding the traditional therapeutic frame in addition to the alterations necessitated by its multiperson circumstance. While matters of confidentiality, trust, anonymity, transference–countertransference, and enactments reconfigure within the expanded frame, underlying hypothetical psychic invariants are retained.

Who Belongs in Group?

Anzieu (2021) defined our task as "finding a psychoanalytic answer to human malaise in our present civilization" (p. 109) and to work wherever "the unconscious arises: standing, sitting or lying down; individually, in a group or in a family; during the session, on the doorstep, at the foot of a hospital bed, etc." (p. 115). Most group psychotherapists assume that individuals who are capable of psychodynamic treatment are suitable for group psychotherapy. We evaluate candidates with an eye to the composition of the group; important variables include age, presenting symptoms, psychological sophistication, diagnosis, ego functioning, severity, and setting, e.g., private practice, clinic, or hospital (see Yalom and Leszcz [2020, pp. 293–355] for an exhaustive discussion). We think psychoanalytically but alter our treatment modality according to the population and setting.

The *in vivo* group experience may be especially valuable for the hard-to-reach individual, the "non-psychologically-minded" who

DOI: 10.4324/9781032703251-6

have difficulty in connecting with their inner lives, or with certain aspects of symbolization as with early trauma (Garland, 2010, p. 20). Linking emotionally to others with similar experiences and participating in group discourse and enactments may bring to light warded, unremembered, or unmentalized experience; a more fully realized psychological being often emerges. People with severe psychological disturbance entwined with socio-economic deprivation "need to construe refuge as a key function of the group…[concerns are with] fundamental levels of survival and belonging and less with analysis" (Nitsun, 2015, p. 110). Informal "coffee and doughnuts" support groups have been effective in stabilizing chronically impaired individuals and lowering the likelihood of (re)hospitalization.

Except for institutional settings requiring mandatory treatment, individuals rarely join a group without some mutual check-out with the leader, so as to establish a rudimentary alliance. Some prospective members may require preparatory or ongoing individual treatment. Prior to entry, members may be accommodated with a conceptual framework and guidelines (Yalom and Leszcz, 2020, pp. 355–375) or encouraged to face their fantasies and expectations in the group itself. In parallel, many group therapists prepare the group for the new member, while others, me for one, tend to privilege ambiguity and explore member responses within the treatment setting.

Before and during the early sessions, it is important to analyze "the resistance to joining the group—in the patient and in me [the therapist]" (Grotjahn, 1977 p. 58). A new member represents aspects of the group leader, as the baby represents aspects of parents. Whereas there may be no such thing as an ugly baby to its parents, therapists may be considerably less charitable in their feelings toward prospective members. The therapist may be proud and wish to show off an attractive, status patient, or to hide one who is neither. Lacan put it thus: "It is ultimately the analyst's desire which operates in psychoanalysis" (cited in Rowan and Harper, 1999, p. 190). The analytically-inclined therapist "desires" group psychotherapy, but not always for all members of one's practice.

After a few consultations, a woman felt she was ready to "take her medicine" and join one of my groups, her expressed intention. "People don't really like me, they respect me." She recalled her senior high school year when she had been voted "Most Likely to Succeed." She longed to be "Most Popular," but was treated as far too serious, and not "really pretty," meaning socially attractive. I realized that I had the same mix of feelings toward her, and that I had projected these feelings onto each of the several potential groups to which I had mentally assigned her. Her acknowledgment of fears and vulnerability not only gave me important insight into her personality but alerted me to heretofore vague countertransference aversion. I now felt more compassion for this woman, and confident that I could facilitate her group placement and minimize unnecessarily painful interactions.

Combined Treatment: A Unified Therapeutic Field

I advocate *combined* individual–group psychotherapy whenever this is feasible. (In contrast to a *conjoint* approach involving concurrent therapies with different therapists.) The *combined modality* provides a unified and intensified therapeutic field in which observation, participation, and interpretation extend beyond each modality in isolation. Stimulating and reviving scenarios of inclusion–exclusion with parents, siblings, and social networks, combined treatment focuses on multiple, as well as mutual, influences. Psychic data – transference, resistance, recovery of trauma, envy and jealousy, regressive and progressive experience – may seem to originate with one treatment modality, or both. The two modalities may be experienced as dialogic, antagonistic, complementary, or hierarchic. Each modality exists separately and perhaps simultaneously in the minds of all group participants, including the therapist.

> Tory: "I told Richard I need to leave group. I'm having another baby and I don't have time to keep all my individual sessions and drive out here for group. Besides, my husband has a new job and I can't count on his being home. Even

though Richard didn't say anything, I know he wants me to stay in group, to keep a good customer."

From members: "How are you planning on feeding the baby?" "Why no time?" "Why don't you get a 'live-in' or more baby-sitting help so you don't have to rely on your husband coming home?"

Tory: "Rich said all this to me, but it didn't sound 'analytic.' I feel he's just manipulating me. I can accept it when it is from you."

Peter (group member, sardonic): "You can't trust Rich, but you trust group, so you want to leave group and spend your time with him?"

Tory: "Yes, exactly. I can't tell what my mother is really thinking. She always has a goal in mind. Like she complains about my sister and brother not visiting her, and I hear the message that I should take better care of her. It makes me want to be close to her, have her all to myself, even though I'm mad at her for being untrustworthy."

Peter (playfully): "I don't trust Rich either. He knows when I'm bullshitting the group, and I don't see him privately."

Tory: "I trust him with you, but not with me."

In the individual sessions that followed, Tory did not bring up the group session or talk about her conflicts about continuing group, nor did I. I had confidence that she would struggle with issues of trust–distrust when, where, and how she wanted to. Several weeks later a member asked: "So are you staying?"

Tory: "I didn't expect such a caring response. You people are so smart. I guess I better. I hired a baby-sitter. I'm going to deduct it from Rich's bill."

The group session provided a *manifest* context for Tory to articulate, explore, and, perhaps, partially repair the trauma of untrustworthy dependency. To some extent, each individual has experienced the failure of maternal provision, which theorists have posited as necessary for psychological separation (Winnicott), reality testing (Freud), and the discovery of the self (Kohut). Given Tory's history of parental neglect and deceit, the "shadow" of bad (internal) objects fell on her intrapsychic and interpersonal relations, impacted both her desire and fear, and constituted an important dimension of her (split) transferences to the therapist, other group members, and the whole group.

Striking was the relationship with "the therapist of the dyad," which left Tory in the predicament of longing to depend on an undependable object. She trusted "the therapist of the group" to provide for other members such as Peter, but not for herself. However, even her professed trust in the group was contradicted by her surprise at its maternal quality: "I didn't expect such a caring response."

I had a parallel response to Tory, not entirely trusting her. Was Tory seriously thinking of leaving group? I did and do not know. I waited to see how, and if, she would negotiate the two fantasy therapists. Due to her identification with and ambivalence towards her unreliable mother, Tory could not trust her own mind sufficiently to develop a coherent view of the therapist and the combined psychotherapy. Peter served as a prominent group *spokesperson* who could think – both rationally and irrationally – and hence represented a caring and dependable figure. Notice that productive psychic derivatives arise from other group members such as Peter, a witness to, but not actual participant in, combined treatment.

It seems disingenuous for a therapist to act as if not in possession of extra-group information acquired from dyadic treatment and is duplicitous to withhold rather than to invite (or even initiate) disclosure of such information when it could be helpful to the member and clarifying for the group. As always, the contents of withheld material are less significant than the member's motivations in withholding.

All individuals exert pressure on the group, and likewise, the group presses on the mentality of each member, the therapist most of all. The "analytic third" gets crowded with others: intersubjective constellations of "fourths," "fifths," and so on. From contemplating the initial interview and onward, we consider the individual as a potential group member, whether an invitation is offered or accepted. For those practicing combined psychoanalytic psychotherapy, the "group" never leaves the consulting room.

Confidentiality and Anonymity

Group psychotherapy moderates the exclusivity of the dyadic relationship. Front and center are issues of confidentiality and trust, although they are not the same. Confidentiality cannot be guaranteed or strictly enforced. While members may believe that their communications are sufficiently confidential, distrust lingers. Few suppose that another individual, much less a family or community, can be entrusted with one's innermost feelings and fantasies. No one presents an unscreened window into their interior life. At one time, to reach the goal of confidentiality, therapists mandated anonymity, with members revealing only their first names. Given contemporary norms relating to e-mail, texting, Google, Facebook, and X (formerly Twitter), members often compile personal data about each other and establish extra-group communication networks. The therapist cannot certify that such communications are shared equally among participants or brought to the group. Depending on the therapist's orientation, types of extra-therapeutic contact may be discouraged, forbidden, explored, or even encouraged, as in the practice of an extra, leader-less group session, at one time a common procedure.

Neutrality, Abstinence, and Self-disclosure

Unless reconceived, certain elements of classical psychoanalysis contribute to a static, "hierarchical arrangement of power and privilege" (Gerson, 1996, p. 626). Gill (1994, p. 50) proposed that "it is the analyst's awareness of this unremitting influence of patient and analyst on each other and his attempt to make that influence as explicit as possible that constitute his 'neutrality'." The classically-oriented psychoanalyst, Ralph Greenson (1967, p. 91) acknowledged that everything therapists "do or say, or don't do or say, from the décor of our office, the magazines in the waiting room, the way we open the door, greet the patient, make interpretations, keep silent, and end the hour, reveals something about our real self and not only our professional self."

Given the reality of unconscious transmission of psychic data, self-disclosure is inevitable and continuous in any human interaction. The lines between intentional and unintentional self-disclosure are ambiguous and fluctuating. The therapist's self-disclosures range from measured revelation to spontaneous exclamation, from those that are seemingly consciously determined to those unconsciously enacted. Subjectivity reveals itself in subtleties of timing, tone, cadence, posture, facial expressions, and gestures, and may contradict what is verbally spoken. Our body speaks, as in smiling, nodding, and looking towards and away. Try as we might, we cannot control tropisms of attraction and repulsion. The dilations of our pupils, the movement of our eyebrows, and the tone of our voice convey varied combinations of empathy and understanding, curiosity, perplexity, and challenge. Like other members, we tense in enduring mental pain and relax in prolonging mental pleasure.

In the tradition of Ferenczi (see Rudnytsky, Bokay, and Giampieri-Deutsch, 1996, and Harold Searles, 1979), some relationally-oriented therapists opt to reveal subjective aspects of themselves purposefully, to model openness, encourage mutual exploration, or take responsibility for their actions and effects on others. In utilizing intentional self-disclosure, one must first evaluate whether it would open things up, a question that may be answered only retrospectively, and even then, without certainty that another way may not have been better (Aron, 1996).

Free Association and Discourse

A grand illusion of psychoanalysis is that free association is inevitably therapeutic and that the analyst's subjectivities need not be considered. In group, the social necessity involves considering the ideas and emotions of many individuals. It is neither possible nor advisable to free associate at all times, and it is questionable whether associations are "free" at all, rather than context bound and a response to the demand characteristics of the analytic process. As the analog to the free-associational process, group interchanges operate as "passing points from one subjectivity to another" (Kaës, 2007, p. 90; also Foulkes, 1975). The discourse process is not a simple matter of member-to-member transmission. No one listens and resounds in the same way, responses are "subjectified" by the developmental history of each member, and by the dynamics of the group and one's roles within it.

Words, Action, Enaction

Freud's (1916/1917, p. 17) assertion that "nothing takes place in a psycho-analytic treatment but an interchange of words between the patient and the analyst" exists in a historical context. *Enactments* – ongoing action scenarios – are inevitable, such that the group situation may be reconceived as an intersubjective enactive "field." Kierkegaard noted: "*Life can only be understood backwards, but it must be lived forwards.*" We may characterize the therapeutic process similarly. Whereas, formerly, actions have been distinguished from thinking, thinking is now regarded as a form of relational action (Greenberg, 1996). *Actual groups* incorporate and *enact* dynamics of each member's *internal groups.*

Gerson (2004, p. 81) described a relational unconscious, which refers to "processes through which individuals communicate with each other without awareness about their wishes and fears, and in so doing, structure the relational unconscious according to both mutually regulated concealments and searches for recognition and expression of their individual subjectivities." Enactments are the "derivatives in action of the relational unconscious" (Gerson, 2004, p. 85).

Therapists may enact purposively with the intent to connect with and affirm a patient, reduce barriers of static *resistances, rebellions*, and *refusals*, and precipitate new or more mature forms of engagement. Greenberg (2018, p. 984) provided a surprising enactment from Melanie Klein, who offered to adjust an analysand's appointment time in order to respond to his anxieties about meeting people in the waiting room; she also extended the sessions when he was very late. To meet a patient's *selfobject* needs, Kohut enacted approving gestures as if to say, "I'm proud of you my boy." "Now that's an interpretation, or at least it is the parallel to the interpretation in psychoanalysis" (Kohut, 1991, p. 533). Lacan caressed an analysand's cheek, a "geste a peau," an enactment that she found transformative (reported by Kirshner, 2015, p. 75), but a gesture we would challenge today as sexist and paternalistic.

Blos (1979) advocated a strategic technique of *guided acting out* as effective with verbally unmotivated adolescents (see also, Billow, 2004b). "A carefully chosen concretization...may substitute for symbolic speech...[to bridge] to perceptions and affects that had not advanced to word representation or were excluded by them by either ego arrest or dissociation" (Blos, 1979, pp. 295–296). Therapeutic initiated enactments can be confrontative yet still manifest empathic "role responsiveness" (Sandler, 1976). As creative "acts of freedom" (Symington, 1983), enactments propel "*now moments*," in which the therapist takes an action novel to the habitual framework to move the treatment forward (D. N. Stern et al., 1998, p. 911).

> To call attention to the increasing number of late joiners, I casually began delaying opening our Zoom sessions. When finally questioned, I claimed innocently to be waiting for a quorum of attendees. "After all, you want a genuine group meeting, don't you?" Members protested and one person (habitually late) deducted a symbolic fraction of the weekly fee. Punctuality resumed with the next session.

Transference–Countertransference

Although Freud (1925, p. 42) frequently referred to transference as a process that develops within the analytic relationship, he offered a wider and remarkably contemporary definition: "Transference is merely uncovered and isolated in analysis. It is a universal phenomenon of the human mind...and in fact dominates the whole of each person's relation to his human environment." Freud, however, did not consider the implications of his broad definition as related to the person of the analyst, similarly constituted. Contemporary psychoanalytic approaches rest on the "common ground" of a hyphenated "transference–countertransference" (Wallerstein, 1990. The communal scope of group treatment elicits multiple intersubjective configurations and multiple transference–countertransferences. Along with those focused on the analyst, member-to-member and member-to-whole group transferences co-exist. Similarly, countertransference extends to members, subgroups, and the group-as-a-whole.

No matter how mindful, every choice of focus exposes the therapist's "conflictual network of associations" (Smith, 2000, p. 124). The therapist's "irreducible subjectivity" cannot be eliminated, and this is not even a desirable goal, as Renik (1993) declared. Boesky (1990, p. 573) asserted that "if the analyst does not get emotionally involved sooner or later in a manner that he had not intended, the analysis will not proceed to a successful conclusion." The goal, then, is not to eradicate our anxieties, resistances, wishes, and fears, but to decrease inhibition and to decrease "the impulse to inhibit" (Bion, 1970, p. 129). While the therapist's conflicts, character structure, and misunderstandings lead to inevitable iatrogenic forces, they also provide vehicles for learning about unconscious relationships and transmitting information.

Reality Testing and Testing Reality

We are trained to help our group members overcome defensive distortions, unrealistic perceptions, and risky behaviors, thus improving their *reality testing*. However, we need also to protect clinical process from premature closure, as when the group becomes involved in overly energetic problem solving. Whether merely in conjectural thought and feeling, or in actual behavior, *testing reality* entails experimentation and risk. When applied to inner life, *testing reality* involves relaxing mentation: clearing the mind of pre-formulated thoughts or typical emotional reactions to allow oneself to "not think." Anything that draws one's attention – feelings/thoughts/fantasies that one may judge as unrealistic, immature, immoral, or primitive – may represent or lead to emotional truth.

Bion (1962, p. 20) drew attention to the difference between solutions to problems and solutions to problems of development. *Testing reality* – working with an individual to solve problems, or a group to reach "enabling solutions" (Whitaker and Lieberman, 1964) may be a first step, an emergent social necessity, or a means of solidifying therapeutic alliances. However, we attempt to extend our reach from merely resolving conflict, to a wider and deeper focus on the growth of the mind and relatedness. When directed by processes of *reality testing*, the group appears coherent and linear in that meaning gradually develops and is clarified. In *testing reality*, the group may be thematically and even behaviorally disorganized, as during certain enactments. The meanings that emerge may seem to arise spontaneously and unpredictably and may co-exist without a drive for consensus or urgent validation. The two types of emotional learning are rarely discrete, particularly in the frame of group wherein all communications are experimental and risk public scrutiny. Just by showing up in a group, members exhibit some willingness to move away from known realities and to involve themselves in something foreign to everyday life. Some individuals dip their toes in unknown waters, some go ankle deep, and some immerse themselves in the flow. It is the therapist's job to make sure no one drowns.

Aggression in Conflict and Growth Models

Metapsychological assumptions about the role of aggression influence the therapeutic frame: how we approach our work with individuals and the group. Freud pit the self's inborn sexual and aggressive instincts against constraining social forces. Bion described the individual as perpetually "at war" with its instinctive groupishness, in order to protect personal identity. According to Lacan and Laplanche, the infant is born into a world of sexual and aggressive desires and "messages." The individual is fated to construct a comprised "stranger" to itself in perpetual conflict with sources unknown.

"Emancipation-oriented" theorists (my term) of different persuasions, some influenced by such forebearers as Marx, Sartre, Foucault, R. D. Laings, Marcuse, Spotnitz, and Winnicott, seek liberation of the "true self" from its false, social self and its maladaptive forms of aggression. In the opposite direction, Foulksian, Lewinian (e.g., Agazarian), Sullivanian (e.g., Yalom and Leszcz) and Kohutian theorists pit the neurotic mind against the group's normalizing forces. They locate aggression in the individual, whose destructive tendencies and defenses create the problems that require a normalizing social group. Kohut-inspired therapists put great value on the group's capacity to supply missing selfobject needs, so as to foster integration and a peaceful resolution of aggressive conflicts. In Foulkes' optimistic view, the corrective emotional experience of group transforms aggressive destructiveness into healthy assertiveness. There is no sense that the group itself, or the community, may be overly conformist, deviant, or destructive (Nitsun, 1996).

In the traditional dyadic frame, overt expressions of aggression are unidirectional, directed from the analysand to the analyst, and communicated via words and symbolic derivatives such as metaphor, fantasy, and dream. In the expanded group frame, expressions of aggression and sexuality among members are multidirectional, often subterranean, irruptive, or disguised by its opposites, as in exaggerated empathy and benevolence.

Regarding the analyst's aggression, these cautionary alerts from Winnicott (1949):

> It seems to me doubtful whether a human child as he develops is capable of tolerating the full extent of his own hate in a sentimental environment. He needs hate to hate. If this is true, a psychotic patient in analysis cannot be expected to tolerate his hate of the analyst unless the analyst can hate him.
>
> (p. 73)

He also advised that however much the analyst loves, "he cannot avoid hating, and the better he knows this the less will hate and fear be the motive determining what he does to his patients" (p. 68). Smith (2000, p. 112) suggested the analyst's aggression is always near at hand: a "benign negative transference," and cautions that ignoring it leads to distraction, sleepiness, masochistic listening, and gratuitous sympathy. Analysts must possess "a certain amount of cruelty" and not be "too nice," Carl Jung declared (in Atlas and Aron 2018, p. 117). The therapist "must not be afraid to love, nor be a stranger to hate" (Grotjahn, 1977, p. 213; see also, Zeisel, 2012, p. 227).

Unrepresented and Unrepresentable States of Mental Experience

Birksted-Breen (2016, p. 5) underscored that "here and now always refers to that which is not apparently there, the unconscious, the lost connection, the absent other, the non-represented." Some of which we deal with is only indirectly discernible, never fully knowable, and can only be approached via intuition and conjecture. The essentials of intrapsychic and interpersonal communication begin and may remain on verbally unarticulated levels in which thinking remains partially undeveloped (Ogden, 1989; Stolorow, Magid, Fosshage, and Shane, 2021). This is the domain of the "unthought known," "unformulated experience" (D. B. Stern, 2019), and the "unrepresentable unconscious" (Levine, 2023). The technical question persists: how we can utilize talk therapy to reach that which exists before language and remains rooted in the body, as "memories in feelings" (Klein, 1957, p. 180).

In *Experiences in Groups*, Bion (1961) first tackled the problem, describing "protomental" phenomena that does not reach the level of fully thinkable thoughts, and similarly, undeveloped "protofeelings." In his later metapsychological writings, Bion postulated the existence of an essential "*alpha-function*," which organizes into conscious and unconscious thoughts these elements of "raw" experience (which Bion labeled as "*beta elements*"). Guided by of *alpha functioning*, conscious and unconscious *mental transformations* (Bion, 1962) produce thinkable thoughts: symbols, nameable feelings, and emotional ideas of increasing complexity. In psychoanalytic treatment, the therapist unitizes a dream-like state of "*reverie*" to "*alphabetize*" *beta elements* (the unrepresented) in order to make them capable of being "contained" by symbolizable thoughts and verbal language (James Grotstein [2002], personal communication; *Chapter 6*).

Bion's semi-mystical dimension of *0*, and Lacan's *Real*, refer to that which we cannot know, only "know about." An analogy in philosophy is Kant's "noumenon" or thing-itself, in contrast to the "phenomenon" of everyday experience, which are mere shadows on the wall of Plato's cave. An "unstructured unconscious" describes that which remains "unthinkable" and unverbalizable. Originating in the (perhaps unavoidable) experiences of a frightened and overexcited infant, overwhelmed with what Klein referred to as *death anxieties*, "an overwhelming frenzy of stimuli inside the mind and body" (Bergstein, 2019, p. 13) threatens to emerge, similar to Bion's description of "*catastrophic anxiety.*"

In "Constructions in analysis," Freud (1937) asserted that a construction – a conjecture or intuition – can stand in and serve the same purpose in the dynamics of the cure as can the recovery of an actual traumatic memory from childhood (in Levine 2022, p. 194). Bion (1987, p. 76) noted that "the analyst has to be an artist—he has to make constructions of what is going on." He described a way of "being with" by "blinding" oneself to the discourse of mature thought to reach intuitive apprehensions. Departing from the group's immediacy and using *reverie*, the therapist spins a "dream" composed of the group's verbal discourse and enactments and personal associations. Reaching a tentative formulation, the therapist may construct, or leave the unsaid as unsaid.

Chapter 5

Group Process

Chapter 5 considers *group forces* ("*G*") and *phases, internal* and *actual groups*, Freud's *primary* and *secondary processes*, Klein's *psychotic* and *normal/neurotic positions*, and Bion's three basic affects, *LHK* (loving, hating, and curiosity). These terms describe states of emotional and cognitive organization through which a group generates and forestalls emotional truths. The *3Rs*, overlapping processes of *resistance, rebellion*, and *refusal*, designate individual and group modes of coping with the meaning-making project. Whether relatively passive, active, or interpretive, the group therapist remains a central figure. To some extent, it is "*all about me*," the therapist.

"*G*": *Group Forces*

Consider this question: How long before a gathering of individuals becomes a group? Kurt Lewin's empirical studies revealed that a "grouping" effect operated almost immediately, even with a collective of strangers and independent of sociological categories. *G* seems to be constitutional and universal. Most of us have experienced the pleasure of being part of a large group and feeling as one, for example at concerts or sporting events. However, we also need to feel separate, even then. When people gather together, grouping and individuation needs operate in tension. Maturational tasks include developing and maintaining one's unique identity, while learning to respect differences.

DOI: 10.4324/9781032703251-7

For, from its preliminary formation, a group stimulates a sense of belongingness, similarity, and antagonism to others (Freud, 1930, p 114; Volkan, 1988). Erikson (1985) hypothesized an evolutionary tendency for "pseudospeciation," identifying only one's own ethnic or social group as "human beings," and all others as less than human. He echoed Freud's (1921) speculation of an "archaic heritage" that resides in our collective memory. *G* is also likely to play a part in tribalism, as when belonging and being loyal to the tribe may override cognitive activity, for example in political identifications. We may see antecedents in the infant's stranger anxiety.

G generates energy from what Lewin and Bion referred to as "*valency*," a rapid formation of group uniformity of thought, feelings, and interactional behavior. (Freud [1921, p. 75] had referred to this dimension as *contagion*.) As laughter increases in a full movie house when compared to a relatively empty one (Koenig and Lindner, 1994), *valency* amplifies emotional reactions. The cover of anonymity and proximity among individuals stimulates contagion of feeling and ideas. *Valency* contributes to the power of the group to stimulate transference and countertransference, as members come to represent a collection with a singular mind and personality.

Comparable to the grounding force of gravity, *G* is pervasive, drawing from intertwined needs for attachment and meaning (Bowlby, 1988). From infancy onwards, we look to others to discover ourselves: "me-ness" cannot be felt or described without some sense of "we-ness." Those who are swept up by *G*, or attempt to pull away, are that much more socially preoccupied, although unsatisfactorily. To utilize *G* productively, the therapist welcomes *G*, surrendering to the shared networks of feeling, fantasy, and thought. To not abuse the group situation, however, the therapist must counter *G*'s forces too, for there are dangers to independent thinking, pressures emanating from the social forces inherent in grouping. Conforming to group norms and expectations provides a sense of identity, regularity, and security for the therapist as well, and therein lies its temptation. When interacting in groups – which is always – there is a press to revert to thinking that is "very simple and very exaggerated...[with] neither doubt nor uncertainty" (Freud, 1921, p. 78, quoting Le Bon).

Group Process: An Imaginary Concept with Experiential Properties

"Group" is an imaginary concept, with a strong experiential base. Existing on an intermediate zone between reality and fantasy, individuals "collect together and form a group on the basis of the similarity of our illusory experience. This is a natural root of grouping among human beings" (Winnicott, 1971, p. 3). From its exterior, group boundaries are relativity fixed by the dimensions of reality: time, place, purpose, and membership. However, from its interior, a group is crisscrossed with multiple *psychic* boundaries, which blur, stratify, and multiply. People and places psychically renew, remodelled in each encounter. Time extends backward and forwards, to the past and future, from "here-and-now" to "there-and-here" and "there and then," to the feared, painful, and disavowed, to the anticipated, wished for, or dreaded. Different personalities and combinations of personalities assert force and counterforce to "co-create" and move events.

"Our therapeutic practice is founded on metaphor" (Powell, 1994, p. 24), as are our concepts of group process. Physical and bodily terms describe abstract social-psychological relationships: *matrix, web, field, boundaries, structure, holding, parallel process, container/contained, homeostasis, role suction, introjection/projection, group-as-a-whole*, and *subgroups*. Experientially we feel process in our guts. Groups have *immediacy, force, velocity, volume, intensity, cadence*, even *taste*, such as *sweet, sour,* or *bitter*. Sensory words describe registers of pleasure–displeasure, fear, anxiety, attraction, and repulsion. The group is *alive, dead, exciting, gripping, calming, warm*, too *hot*, or too *cold*. A host of conceptual networks encode and organize our assumptions linguistically.

Phases of Group

In *linear and diachronic models*, such as Freud's psychosexual stage formulation, mental growth progresses along certain irreversible developmental lines in which the individuals acquire mental maturity. In *synchronic models*, such as Klein's scheme of interacting psychic "positions," dialectic relations develop between different stages and structures of mental development, some remaining infantile, others more mature.

No groups, and few therapists, strictly adhere to a linear stage model (Agazarian being the exception). Groups and individuals cycle through *psychic phases*. "Hermeneutic spirals" (Gayle, 2009) of meaning-making ensue. In Bion's model, for example, a shifting balance of *workgroup* and *basic assumption* mental processes vitalizes or stultifies the group. Tuckman's (1965) well-known stage model of group development emerged from the study of short-term groups (Bonebright, 2010). I consider his rubric, "forming, storming, norming, performing and adjourning" as *states of mind*. As such, they represent feelings, fantasies, and action tendencies expressed in discourse and in subtle and overt enactments that reappear throughout the group's life.

Still, stage models may be useful to "anchor" and direct the therapist to carry out specific tasks as the group evolves. Rutan, Stone, and Shay (2014, pp. 44–66) proffered a four-stage model: *formative, reactive, mature*, and *termination*, which they analogized to processes of individual development. The *formative* stage, in which the group is "birthed," involves establishing attachment and trust. In the *reactive* stage, members practice independence, returning to the leader periodically for nurturance and support. The reactive phase may involve "storming" or rebellion and be like a toddler's "terrible twos." *Mature* and *termination* stages, analogous to adolescent and young adult individual development, share similarities with Bion's *workgroup* in which discourse and enactions come to be understood on multiple levels, including the *symbolic*.

A new group turns to its leader for stability and direction while developing its own *idioms*, aesthetic patterns of being (Bollas, 1987) that characterize each group's unique culture and process. Long term, "open groups," wherein new members replace departed ones, may briefly recapitulate characteristics of a beginning phase, marked by awkward silences, chatter, interrogation, or the group's revaluation of itself. Who are we, what are we about? Dormant issues and conflicts reemerge: dependency, sexual and/or sibling rivalry, and competition for special attention. "I don't want to share you with even more people," a member complains. "I resent having to start over again." "Perhaps this is a good time for me to terminate, you brought in a replacement." New members reawaken the excitement and resentments in greeting a new sibling and the stranger anxiety in confronting an unknown other. Still, idiomatic patterns tend to reassert themselves.

> In a group of eight members, three of the four men dominated with strong, outgoing personalities. The four women rationalized their passivity by claiming that the group reflected the sexist culture of our society and implicated my male complicity. I supported the perspectival truth of their accusations, although I thought I had monitored my gender-based biases. The addition of two outspoken females did not alter the overarching idiom involving two "cultural" subgroups. They sparred with the three dominant men, while the five others remained resentful and subsidiary. Since the group's cleavage no longer hinged on obvious gender lines, I felt I could pursue underlying self-object identifications and projections. The reticent members revealed family prototypes of aggression and submission unrelated to stereotypical gender characteristics. This led to explorations of self-defeating attention-getting mechanisms (Billow, 2019) involved in social withdrawal and underlying motives of resentment, retaliation, spite, and envy. The talkative members retrieved vague feelings of guilt for "being alive." An enlivening redistribution of verbal expressiveness emerged slowly and only partially, requiring my patience and frequent encouragement.

The Interplay of Mental Categories

Referring both to individual and group experience, Bion (1961, p. 159) described "two different categories of mental activity" that co-exist. "The painful bringing together of the primitive and the sophisticated...is the essence of the developmental conflict" (p. 172) and the crux of our work. In introducing the concepts of the pleasure and reality principles, Freud (1911; 1915b) previously had elaborated a two-state model of "primary" and "secondary" process thinking. The former, irrational, emotional, and imaginative, expresses sexual and aggressive desires. The later, in contrast, is rational, logical, and realistic, a product of mental development and adaptive defences involving repression and sublimation (A. Freud, 1981). Following her father's epigenetic formulation of oral, anal, phallic, latency, genital phases, Anna Freud maintained that development proceeded with an irreversible progression of stages, in which *primary process* thinking is gradually relinquished for *secondary processes.*

In contrast, and without naming it as such, Klein (1952) devised a *multiple* self-state model. Developmentally early *"psychotic positions,"* dominated by paranoid-schizoid and depressive phantasies, anxieties and defences, function in dynamic interaction with higher-level mental organization typical of *normal-neurotic* thinking. Extending Klein's formulations to include the group, Bion described the three *basic assumptions*; these rely on Klein's *psychotic defences of splitting and projection.* The *workgroup*, analogous to the *neurotic/normal* part of the personality, relies on logic, verbal formulation, and insight. In productive circumstances under the auspices of its leader, the *basic assumptions* and *workgroup* interact, each energizing and supplying information to the other. A psychoanalytic group culture is marked by this interplay – "the painful coming together" of the irrational and rational.

Benefitting from Sullivan's model of dissociation but also informed by British object relations thinking, Bromberg (2009) characterized the mental apparatus as organized on a dynamic dissociative–integrative continuum that reconfigures according to the evocative potential of the current interpersonal moment. Interactive, autonomous *suborganizations* of internalized self and object representations move in and out of consciousness. Interpersonalists align with Bromberg's assumption that "problems in living" (Sullivan's phrase) reflect destructive interpersonal events linked to developmentally early emotional experience. In mental disturbance, dissociative phenomena persist, limiting or foreclosing the capacity to hold and reflect upon different states of mind. New meaning emerges from the discovery and integration of isolated, split-off, or undeveloped aspects of the self (Davies, 1999; Hoffman, 1994; D. B. Stern, 2019), a project that may be carried out jointly by the therapist and the group.

Bucci (2021), a psychoanalytically-oriented cognitive-developmentalist, presented a *multiple code* model of thinking. Two primary forms operate continuously: *subsymbolic* and *symbolic* (*symbolic verbal* and *symbolic nonverbal*). *Subsymbolic* systems constitute the affective core that accounts for a sense of self across various emotional contexts. For all group members, "preoperational," "non-declarative," "implicit," "procedural memory systems" function in conjunction with the "explicit," "declarative" symbolic levels of logic and reflective thought and language.

"Internal Groups" and Actual Groups

Group dynamics operate with each person coping with "internal objects" that form "*internal groups.*" Often unconscious or dissociated, internal groups influence how one experiences real-world or *actual* groups. Internal groups are polyphonic; the "voices" consist of images, scenes, memories, feelings, and fantasies from different developmental epochs, superimposed on each other and reconfigured ongoingly. They are populated by intergenerational "enigmatic messages" (Laplanche, 1999) that trigger *unconscious alliances* and *misalliances* among members of the actual group (Kaës, 2007). Some internal groups are "intersubjective," shared by many members, while others are "intrasubjective," unique to each individual. All of us have received early messages such as "listen to your parents," "be nice," or "you're in trouble." How these messages were communicated – their force, context, and clarity – and by whom – have shared as well as unique biographical and subcultural resonance. Each participant communicates as an individual and as the group's "speech bearer" of shared internal groupings and attendant sexual and aggressive fantasies, anxieties, and defences (Kaës, 2007).

LHK: Three Basic Affects or Drives; "Plus" or "Minus"

While Bion continues to inspire contemporary psychoanalytic thinking, his ideas on human emotion get little attention and are not well known. Drawing on Platonic and Kantian epistemology, Bion posited that the human being has an inborn knowledge of its emotional needs but lacks the mental development to deal with them. Interestingly, Freud also hypothesized the existence of pre-existing structures of emotional experience. He defined affects as "reproductions of very early, perhaps even pre-individual, experiences of vital importance" and compared them to "universal, typical and innate hysterical attacks" (Freud, 1926, p. 133).

While Freud (1905, p. 194) had acknowledged the "instinct for knowledge or research," he did not consider curiosity basic to one's constitutional equipment and dated its onset to the Oedipal phase. Klein described a powerful "epistemophilic instinct" that, from birth, drives phantasies and relationships, but she did not integrate it into a metapsychology. Revising dual-instinct theory in the light of Klein's new emphasis, Bion posited a third drive overarching the sexual and aggressive: the urge to think and find meaning. He notated three primary drives as *LHK*: to love, to hate, and to seek knowledge (particularly emotional knowledge). These constitutional or instinctual givens provide the psychic stimuli of emotional experience. Babies want the breast, push it away, and explore it too. Adults treat their experience similarly. Affects of "yum!" (*L*), "yech!" (*H*), and "mmm?" (*K*) pass through us second-by-second as we get through our day.

However, because these primal affects are need-dominated, the emotional information *LHK* convey may be judged as "not nice," too needy, sexual, aggressive, or primitive. An upsurge of "yum," "yech," or "mmm" often conflicts with the wish to see oneself – and to be seen by others – as mature, in control, and moral in thought as well as in deed. As they emerge, *basic affects* may be accompanied by *premonitory anxiety*, a state of warning and even dread (Bion, 1961). In this premonitory state, affects may be disavowed and left without further development; thoughts may be uttered, or emotions may be expressed, but they are formulaic and lifeless, without deep personal meaning. In effect, a group in this shared state of mind has nothing to think about, except to think about that.

The quality of one's thinking about affects – the movement of *K* over the fields *L* and *H* – defines the quality of relatedness. The crucial dimension of *LHK* is *plus* or *minus*. Any affect may further or hinder emotional links. *K* exists as itself, and also as a superordinate organizing force of *LHK*. When two or more group members discuss mutual resentments openly and nondefensively, this is +*H*. When empathy is excessive, it pre-empts and constricts other affects; this is -*L*. Curiosity functions as -*K* when intrusive or obsessional.

Tomkins (1995) listed nine positive and negative affects varying from mild to extreme that can be regrouped under Bion's *plus/ minus* rubric. For instance, anger, which Tomkins categorized as a "negative affect," has positivity (+*H*), conveying information (*K*) about unattended needs and hurts that require repair (*L*). Conversely, Tomkins' list of "positive" affects may not be so; an excess of the groups' "interest-excitement" may flood the speaker with too many expressed feelings and opinions (-*L*,-*H*,-*K*).

Like other members, the therapist may be "taken over" by a *basic affect* and misidentify or exaggerate the influence of a *basic assumption*. For example, a therapist may undubly fear personal or group destruction (-*H*) when members express anger (*fight/flight*). Or, perplexed by the group's competing attention-getting pursuits, the therapist neglects unmet individual and collective +*L* longings (*dependency*). Feeling rejected when a group seems to ignore the therapist's thoughts (-*H*), the therapist may abandon the leadership role, withdrawing spitefully, leaving members to "cure" themselves (*pairing*). Individuals gauge their therapist's toleration for loving and being loved, for hating and being hated, for knowing and coming to be known.

(1) An individual in combined treatment casually commented: "I like you better in group, you're more fun. You look like you're enjoying yourself and not working so hard." I assessed (*K*) internally whether I was enjoying myself too much in group (-*K*), or too little in our dyad (-*L*).

(2) A socially isolated young man new to group, commented: "I'm afraid of you in group. You seem impatient with me." The group silently concurred. I first considered that his perception of my impatience related to my anxiety to protect him (+*L*) from my anticipation of the group's lack of interest in his flat and lengthy narratives (-*K*). However, the group "adopted" their youngest member and remained tolerant (+*L*) and curious (+*K*). I had projected onto the group my negative feelings and

acted them out (-*H*). His forthright acknowledgment of my intolerance restored my interest in our relationship (+*LHK*).

Emotion is the result of our affective biography (Nathanson, 2008) and, therefore, has a social dimension. Affects are basic, but thinking about and expressing affects is scripted by our experience with affects; our own and those around us. The more vulnerable affects like fear, shame, anger, or distress are treated with compassion in some families and are scorned as weakness in others. The questions "what are you feeling?" or "what thoughts/associations are you having?" may be steps in the discovery process, but they cannot be answered conclusively, and they may mislead (*Chapter 6*). In group and elsewhere, subterranean combinations of contrary and antagonistic motive forces (and defences against them) play out. Shifts between so-called positive and negative affects are constant; and curiosity about them determine group process.

The 3Rs: Resistance, Rebellion, and Refusal

I have introduced three overlapping constellations of group life and group process: *resistance, rebellion*, and *refusal* (Billow, 2010a). These refer to demeanors, tensions, and actions that are hypothetical, and not discrete, and that may appear different to different observers. These dynamics exist on the intrapsychic or individual level, in dyadic or subgroup relationships, and as phasic group processes. Individuals and groups resist, rebel, or refuse for all sorts of motives, including many that are reasonable. Further, the patterns may serve as an impetus to independent thinking and new modes of relating. Hence, these categories do not refer to inherently positive or negative qualities, or to a particular outcome. For instance, a highly resistant group member may drop out prematurely, minimally participate, or put a pall on group interactions, while rebellious or even refusing members may commit energetically to the process and valuably model expanded options of social behavior.

As I consider *rebellion* and *refusal* as ongoing modes, and not necessarily a group stage or indication of combativeness, my conceptualization is at some variance with certain ideas of "resistance" and "rebellion" as it has figured in major theories of group process (e.g., Freud, 1921; Bion, 1961; Bennis and Shepard, 1956; Agazarian, 1997; Ormont, 1992). Freud (1913) utilized myth to describe how groups, in the aftermath of a murderous rebellion against the primal father (who took all the women for himself), guiltily massed under a new father figure, and established principles and practices to normalize interpersonal relations. In Freudian theory, group members must work through unconscious resistance to feel and verbalize their wishes to overthrow the leader and indulge their sexual and aggressive fantasies.

Resistance as an Umbrella Term

Freud considered *resistance* to be "anything in the words and actions of the analysand that obstructs his gaining access to his unconscious" (Laplanche and Pontalis, 1973). *Resistance* was "a trial of patience for the analyst (Freud, 1914, p. 155), a "struggle" (1912b, p. 102), since "the resistance accompanies the treatment step by step. Every single association, every act of the person under treatment must reckon with the resistance" (1912b, p. 103). As our techniques have evolved, so too has our understanding of resistance, our relative comfort with its manifestations, and our likely role in its manifestations and working through. Still, *resistance* continues to be used as a wide theoretical umbrella. Too wide, in my opinion, applied colloquially to divergent clinical situations that call for different types of therapeutic interactions.

Resistance may be investigated without the boundaries placed by uncritical acceptance of certain of Freud's metaphors and metapsychological assumptions. While unconscious processes such as *resistance* underlie all mental activity, pressing relationship issues may first need to be addressed. Freud linked resistance to the analyst's *role* as stimulus for resistance (e.g., for the reemergence of unconscious Oedipal fantasies). We now include the analyst's *actual behaviors* as influencing factors. To give a prominent example, Freud attributed *resistance* to "blockages" of "free association" when a patient stopped talking, taking part meaningfully, or claimed to have nothing to say. Individuals, however, have reasons for not talking that are conscious yet uncomfortable, since they implicate their analyst's person, techniques, or behavior.

Such relational data may need to be addressed prior and in addition to unconscious processes. The clinical data may be better approached as a *rebellion* agains*t* or *refusal* to participate within the boundaries of certain demands and constraints that are transmitted by the therapist.

The *3Rs* are intrapsychic and interpersonal regulators. Each describes a type of intersubjective give-and-take; they vary in intentionality, combativeness, and openness to dialogue. The therapist has a stake in the configurations of the *3Rs* and in their persistence and resolution. Let us briefly consider each of them from a relational point of view.

Resistance

Freud (1916/17, p. 451) declared that "to effect cure, advance development, and assure mental health, the therapist must expose and get rid of [resistance]." In "lifting internal resistances…the patient's mental life is permanently changed, is raised to a high level of development and remains protected against fresh possibilities of falling ill" (Freud, 1916/17, p. 451). However, *resistance* cannot be "gotten rid of" or "lifted." Its manifestations can be explored as to underlying meanings and the relationship to the repressed or dissociated past. *Resistance* is as good as it gets. It is the communicative field in which *symbolic* communications predominate.

Resistance reveals meaning gradually, through disguise and indirection: dream, metaphor, symptom formation, transference–countertransference, and enactment. Introspection and retrospection are part of the exploratory/discovery process. The group veers away from the "here-and-now" to consider the "here and then" and the "there and then." In group, members and not only the therapist are potential explorers of resistance, for "everyone possesses in his unconscious mental activity an apparatus which enables him to interpret other people's reactions" (Freud, 1915, p. 15).

Resistance analysis is the fulcrum of a psychoanalytic approach to group therapy: I offer five assertions:

1 Resistance regulates the development, expression, and use of emotional truth.

2 Resistance is motivated by the basic conflict between thinking and not thinking.
3 Resistance reveals interplay between truth and falsity as well as between unconsciousness and consciousness.
4 Resistance involves multiple levels and types of intersubjective interplays, including transference–countertransference.
5 Resistance is not "lifted" – it works towards and away from truth and is continuous.

Rebellion

Members feel intersubjective tensions that arise from differences in beliefs about how their group should function, and at times they rebel against the group process. Usually, the therapist is implicated, and *rebellion* challenges therapeutic assumptions and values, and the therapist's methodology in realizing them. *Rebellion* denotes a strategy of social action, adopted by a faction, when other avenues of influence seem futile or unattractive, a judgment that depends on the therapist's receptivity to discussion and change and equally, on the state of mind of the rebelling faction.

While *rebellion* represents a mental attitude, it is useful to think of it as an attempt to move the group in a different direction. The conflict of therapeutic assumptions and values leading to rebellion may exist quite apart from *resistance*, character dynamics, or transference–countertransference per se. *Rebellion* might represent reasonable differences in beliefs in what constitutes an effective group experience. Exposing and discussing the differences in perspectives, and what are believed to be incongruities in underlying or basic values, become essential to productive group processes. In the current political climate (worldwide), issues of diversity, inclusion, and equality (DEI) may come to the fore and remain as an unresolvable source of tension. Psychodynamic issues underlying perceived and actual inequities may be linked to underlying psychodynamics, in due course, if at all.

When the group cannot resolve or live with dissent, *rebellion* takes various action pathways: *defiance, secession/exile, revolution*, and *anarchy*. While differentiated by their processes and outcomes, each offers a resolution of conflict such that the group may continue to thrive.

This is, however, not so with *anarchy*, a toxic form of *rebellion* (Billow, 2010b). In group processes of *anarchy* and for those individuals anarchy-inclined, disruption and disintegration are tactics, endpoints, and triumphs. The Greek root of anarchy is "without a ruler." On the macro or social level, anarchy seeks to render the leader powerless and without authority, such that a group devolves into disorder and confusion, without cohesive principles and constructive purposes. On the micro or intrapsychic level, anarchy attacks the internal ruler – the mind – to render useless the capacity to order emotional experience and think. The goal is to destroy the particular group, and also, the very idea of group, which is envied and hated. (See also interrelated concepts of *anti-thinking, minus K, attacks on links*, and *parasitic container–contained* relationships (*Chapter 6*).)

Refusal

Refusal establishes a mental boundary between what is considered appropriate and inappropriate for discourse. Certain psychological investigations may be experienced as ill-timed, invasive, or destructive. Whether in silence, words, or action, interest in or expression of psychic material remains sparse, repetitive, or perfunctory. Working with *refusal* requires appreciating how and why certain mental operations are halted or left unspoken. In modes of *resistance* and *rebellion*, the group becomes immersed in conflict and process, *refusal* engenders intellectual void. Emotional material may seem too toxic to touch without the right gloves (Slonim, in Billow, 2021a) or the right person, and may need to be left unaddressed for an interval or longer.

All communication has an element of *refusal*. Rarely are questions directed to the therapist's person answered frankly, and this begins with the response to a member's greeting of "how are you?" Even when being intentionally self-disclosing, the therapist may avoid acknowledging other aspects of personal experience (Greenberg, 1995). A strategy of refusal may partake in any of Bion's three *basic assumptions*. Yet, refusal remains a valid option for the *workgroup* as well, as in establishing or maintaining boundaries, limit setting, protecting privacy, or defying unrealistic or unethical requests or expectations. Nicholas Rescher (1987, p. 9), the philosopher of science, questioned whether "there are things we ought not to know on moral grounds." As a society, we debate whether certain explorations in the realm of nuclear physics or genetic biology represent a search for truth that far exceeds our moral capabilities of using it. Thus, *refusal* may signify a conscious and well-thought-out decision.

Group vs Therapist-centered Group Processes

Yalom (1995, p. 216) presented the maxim: "Unlike the individual therapist, the group therapist does not have to be the axle of therapy. In part, you are midwife to the group: you must set a therapeutic process in motion." Along this line of thinking, Foulkes recommended trusting the group, which will ultimately know how to treat itself. The group therapist "does not step down but lets the group, in steps and stages, bring him down to earth… [the group] replaces the leader's authority" (Foulkes, 1964). In contrast, Bion (1961) concluded that a group without true leadership picks its most disturbed member to lead!

In my opinion, if a group seems "group-centered," it is because its members are following the therapist's directives, leaving unaddressed the dynamics implied by their compliance. "Patients come to group because of the therapist's importance…as an object of cathexis and dependence," Slavson (1957/1992, p. 179) insisted. And from Foulkes (1964, p. 179): "[The group conductor's] influence on the therapeutic group, quite particularly from unconscious sources, is hard to overestimate." In his groundbreaking group work in the 1940s, Bion (1961) observed an intense preoccupation with his personality, interpersonal skills, and overall fitness for leadership, and came to understand how they contributed to the fluctuations of *basic assumptions*.

To emphasize the centrality and continuity of therapist influence, I have facetiously described group process as being "All About Me" (Billow, 2012a; 2012b). Attitudes from and towards the leader influence whatever is being said and all that is left unsaid. At those very moments a group seems to attend to anything and anyone but the leader, he or she likely is of prime interest. Perhaps out of allegiance to group-as-a-whole approaches and the frequent admonition to let the group do the work, therapists may be afraid to draw attention to themselves. Yet, this old joke: "Well, enough of 'me.' Let's hear about you. What do *you* think of me?" Group members tell us what they think about "me" and who we symbolize, via verbal derivatives (metaphors, dreams, jests), enactments, and displacements on to other members.

> Flare-ups quickly developed between two women, one recently introduced to our group, over a particular seat close to mine. After weeks of unproductive group discussions about democracy and seniority and who "deserved" any favored seat, I wearily stated: "they're not fighting over the seat, they're fighting over me." Dispiritedly, both members began to explore their relationships to siblings and fathers. Impatient with the women's intellectualized retrospections, a male member interjected: "You both have a crush on him!" Not wishing to leave the women alone, blindsighted and embarrassed, I added: "Only two! What about the rest of you? I read in my psychology books that every patient is supposed to fall in love with their therapist." "I do [have a crush]" the same man rejoined, adding a few explicit fantasies which, while ignored, led to a lively discussion about how and if people were attracted to me.

The sexually-tinged competitive tension between the two women did not resolve. However, turning attention to "me" opened an enlarged, imaginative context populated by other relationships as well – inner and historical as well actual and current. Relationships stimulated by "me" underlie and reoccur in the group context and relate both to the "real relationship" (Greenson, 1967) and to transference(s).

Chapter 6

Vertical and Horizontal Vectors

Siblings are always part of the therapeutic process: those who wait outside the consulting room and those within. A sibling paradigm keeps horizontal vectors on the therapist's mind, contributing to a decrease of group intervals of deadness, stalemates, and even treatment failure. Take, for example, Guntrip's (the British psychoanalyst) report on his successive analyses with Fairbairn and Winnicott. Neither analyst successfully addressed Guntrip's puzzling series of incapacitating illnesses following the deaths of friends and colleagues. At age 70, he broke through amnesia surrounding the events of his younger brother's death at Guntrip's age of three-and-a-half. The displaced memories of the "repressed idea" of his brother exerted "an unconscious pull out of life into collapse" (Guntrip 1975, p. 150).

Freud's View

Freud conceptualized a sibling complex without naming it as such, and it entered his interpretations (1905, p, 194ff; 1937, p. 261). However, he positioned the developmentally late-appearing Oedipal complex (age three) as coordinating object relationships and delegated sibling relations as displacements. From Freud's perspective, a group is like a traumatized family, held together partially by Eros (loving forces) and partially by reaction formations against envy and aggression towards other members (symbolic younger siblings):

> The fact that the younger child is loved by the parents as much as he himself is...he is forced into identifying himself with the older children...What appears later on in society in the shape of...'group spirit' does not belie its derivation from what was originally envy...This social feeling is based upon the reversal of what was a hostile feeling into a positive-toned tie in the nature of an identification.
>
> (Freud, 1921, p. 120)

However ambivalent, we need and love siblings: they serve as extensions of ourselves and are hated as our replacements (J. Mitchell, 2003). Dylan Thomas (1954, p. 12) captures the ambivalent nature of the sibling experience in this brief excerpt: "It snowed last year too: I made a snowman and my brother knocked it down and I knocked my brother down and then we had tea." The infant fascinates on peers; likewise, the group member. A group brings out positive aspects in sibling relations, such as helping with peer, courtship, and sexual affiliation, and offering protection when aggressing against ("knocking down") the perceived or actual shortcomings of others, including the therapist.

Psychoanalysis Suffers a Sibling Complex

Rapheal-Leff (1990, p. 325) suggested that the death of Freud's younger brother, Julius, has haunted psychoanalytic theory and organizations, both of which remain "encapsulated as an unprocessed wordless area of prehistoric deathly rivalry and identification." While Freud (1925) omitted mention of his seven siblings in his autobiopic sketch, his thinking regarding a fraternal trauma extended into his self-analysis. He diagnosed himself as suffering neurotic "survivor guilt" regarding his brother's death, which occurred when Freud was 18 months old (and thus pre-Oedipal in the Freudian developmental schemata). Freud's relationship with his half-brother's son, one year older than Sigmund, became the model for intimate peer relations:

> I can only say shortly that der Alte [my father] played no active part in my case...I greeted my brother (who was a year

my junior and died after a few months) with ill-wishes and genuine childish jealousy, and that his death left the germ of self-reproaches in me. I have also long known the companion of my evil deeds between the ages of one and two. It was my nephew, a year older than myself...This nephew and this younger brother have determined what is neurotic, but also what is intense, in all my friendships.

(Freud, 1896b, Letter 70, pp. 261–262)

The father of the Oedipal complex minimized his father's impact on his interpersonal conflicts. Freud was a competitive, jealous, and intolerant brother who dominated his five sisters in place of his weak father (Kahn 2014, pp. 46–47). Agger (1988, p. 12) speculated that Freud's formulation of the Oedipus complex – in addition to its scientific merits – represented a neurotic displacement from siblings to parents, sparing Freud of his intense primitive feelings towards his siblings. He speculated that the contemporary analyst, rife with competitive strivings with colleagues, might find sibling countertransference realizations more threatening than vertical, parent-based formulations. Kieffer (2014) suggested that sibling phenomena may be disavowed because their acknowledgment and examination would threaten the hierarchical power structure that remains inherent in psychoanalytic treatment.

Enduring individual and institutional defences of dissociation and denial attest to the intergenerational influence of Freud's sibling complex and could explain its omission from technical theory and practice: "Psychoanalysis still retains the marks left on its concepts and technique by its antidepressant origins (this being understood as [Freud's] neurotic depression): a fairly remarkable intolerance to comprehend and handle, even after Melanie Klein, the paranoid-schizoid position" (Anzieu, 2021, p. 110).

Kaës' Dual Axes Theory

Most contemporary psychoanalysts date the formation of *primary internal groupings* prior to the Oedipal period. Kaës followed Lacan's (1938) model which, per Klein, emphasized two successive developmental stages that contribute to an early or pre-Oedipal complex (Klein, 1952) and inaugurate also the "sibling complex." In contrast to the traditional or Freudian Oedipal triangle, in which the competing figure is the opposite sex parent, Lacan's pre-Oedipal triangle involves mother–infant–phallus, the "phallus" standing for the "*Other*," the fantasied *object of the mother's desire* (Benhaim, 2008; Chiesa, 2007).

The earliest "weaning" stage revolves around the harmonious symbiotic relationship between the newborn and mother, the traumatic separation process, and the infant's consequent feelings of abandonment. The following "intrusion" or "fraternal" stage presents the child with another trauma, the reality of an "other." To the child's horror, it discovers that the mother desires another "little thing like me," a "mirror." The intrusion trauma occurs independent of actual siblings. It is the dawning reality of many "like mes" that raises fears and fantasies of not being cared for and loved. Freud (1937, p. 261) spoke to this realization, although he dated a later origin: "Then came another baby and brought you grave disillusionment." Winnicott (1965, p. 50) described the same situation, in which "something happened, after which nothing was the same again."

It does happen again in every group session. Groups camouflage a collective loss of identity, a loss the leader also feels and must cope with. In the group, the pre-Oedipal rival is the figure of any other, whether a symbolic sibling or parent, the group-as-a-whole, or the outside world: a something or someone turning the desired therapist away from offering exclusive concentration. We mourn the loss of exclusive claims on love and attention and struggle to recover from the fantasy that we ever had it (Lacan's *jouissance*).

Kaës' dual track theory asserts that two axes of pre-Oedipal and early sibling complexes structure the unconscious and hence, *internal groups* and *actual groups*. The "two axes intersect, they conflict, attract one another and sometimes hamper one another, but neither can fully exist without the other" (Kaës, 1993, p. 308, in Benhaim, 2008, p. 263; see also, Levin, 2008; Kirshner, 2006; Tubert-Oklander, 2011). In the *actual group*, organized clusters of pre-Oedipal, fraternal, and Oedipal fantasies, wishes, and fears spur rivalry, curiosity, attraction, and rejection. Representing symbiotic, sexual, masochistic, aggressive, fratricidal, parricidal, matricidal, and cannibalistic fantasies and urges (Kaës, 2007), they are repressed, and also disavowed, dispersed, projected, and enacted collectively. In our *internal groups*, we inherit, inhabit (embody), and project onto others multiple roles: Oedipus, Laius, Jocasta and Antigone, Moses, Cain and Abel, Joseph, and Joseph's brothers.

> In an intensive psychoanalysis, a young man came to recognize his ongoing tension in the presence of his formidable parents and contentious siblings. According to him, I was more like the attentive sports coaches, teachers, and friends he could trust. No matter my approach, it was difficult to access a negative transference, and neither of us wanted to artificially manufacture one. Joining a group, this gregarious young man seemed to lose all self-assurance and stayed in the background. A persistent transference emerged to the group as composed of envious siblings and a dictatorial father–critical mother group leader. In our dyadic work, I continued to be the compassionate "teacher-coach" who helped him understand his unfolding group transferences. In group, our trusting relationship partially dissolved. He dared not challenge my authority or confront what he saw as a coterie of obsequious members. Although he knew better intellectually and could offer no evidence to support his pervasive fantasy, he maintained the emotional conviction that he really wasn't very important to me, and that I preferred others. Treacherous group members replicated competitive brothers and sisters. Gradually, he developed confidence to risk what he felt to be precarious group relationships. When he dared to speak, he discovered a warm reception and respect for his candidness. As a group "speech bearer," he disrupted the members' "unconscious defensive alliances," bringing to the fore the group's warded off Oedipal and sibling anxieties and fantasies. One wonders whether the analytic treatment could have produced such emotional understanding and personal growth for him as well as other members without the addition of the group.

Juliet Mitchell (2003, p. 11) asserted that before siblings "are equal in their sameness to each other for their father, children must be equal in their difference from each other for their mother. This will be the first vertical relation for siblings." In actuality, children are not equal to parents, whose unconscious complexes are variously stimulated (Laplanche, 1999). Likewise, group analysts do not relate to each member equally. Reviving allegiances to our own vertical and horizontal developmental complexes, we may rehash our own reveries in the process of translating others'.

While a generous and empathic figure, George could be abstract and difficult to follow. He acknowledged that the group's reflections meant more to him than his own. As the oldest child in a strict military family, he had been assigned the role of big brother to the five siblings that followed. Under watchful parental eyes, he subjugated his identity and modelled a pattern for his siblings to follow. Whenever the group began to focus on his family relationships, he flared with an otherwise unexpressed anger bordering on moral outrage. "You're piling on, not listening to what I'm saying, taking it way too far." They were grave limits to what could be said and who could say it. Although I felt affection for George, I came to resent that only I, the "group parent," could be the messenger of psychic truth.

In one session, I came to the startling realization that George was not only a symbolic son, but also a dissociated, Jungian "shadow" of me. He was an exaggeration of what I had wished to be and could not tolerate being: a well-behaved child. Indeed, my mother's "why can't you behave like your brother?" stays with me, shared now with some ironic pleasure with my actual brother. I was fortunate, however, to have "chums" (Sullivan's term for "near siblings"), irreverent cousins and schoolmates (none of whom met my parents' full approval). They shared my skeptical views of parents and authority figures, and partially freed me from their control.

Retranscribing the "Container-Contained"

Sibling dynamics enter the analytic register. Bion's symbolic representation [♀♂] ideographically represents *multiple* configurations of psychoanalytic co-participation, encompassing internal, dyadic, triadic, group, and societal interactions. The group functions under the Oedipal laws of the Mother (J. Mitchell) and Father (Lacan). However, to avoid naive historiography, the therapist must attend to the "lawless" residues that reside in the subterranean currents that drive narratives, discourse, and enactments.

The group leader's role is twofold: participating as a containing force and as one of the contained. In some encounters, we function as a benevolent maternal figure who *holds* the group and encourages bonding. At other moments, we *contain* the group, being the symbolic father who encourages thinking and verbal language (Lacan). Yet there is also a sibling dimension. Sitting amid "like mes," the therapist should feel like a *peer* and at times be treated as one. He or she needs to play and allow oneself to be played with, enjoying the group and appreciating members as valued equals sharing an adventure in emotional learning.

In upholding a traditional vertical relationship to the group, the leader reinforces an idealized fantasy of the analyst-parent as "pillar of the faith" (Lacan, 1977, p. 219), an unwavering model and enforcer of appropriate thought and behavior. A group is not so different from the immature child who, through successive developmental stages, needs adults to follow and also, to separate from and engage with peers. The mother "pushes the toddler way from the family and into the peer-group" (J. Mitchell, 2013 p. 5). Likewise, does the group therapist. In doing so, we cannot fully shield group members from growing pains and the inevitable fraternal struggles.

An elaborated version of the *container-contained* expands our technical options, clarifying how we may shift our symbolic boundaries. Viewing ourselves as a maternal and paternal Oedipal containing force and also as a sibling contained with other siblings in the group provides a type of "binocular vision." Bion reserved the ocular metaphor for the analyst, but members are equipped with binocular vision too. Veering into our sibling and Oedipal complexes, they see us up close. We meet others with infiltrating sibling and Oedipal complexes; others receive us with theirs.

Nachtraglichkeit

In his famous letter to Fleiss, Freud (1896a, p. 233) introduced the concept of *"nachtraglichkeit"* (or "afterwardness"):

> I am working on the assumption that our psychic mechanism has come into being by a process of stratification: the material present in the form of memory traces being subjected from time to time to a *rearrangement* in accordance with fresh circumstances—to a *retranscription*...The successive registrations represent the psychic achievement of successive epochs of life. At the boundary between two such epochs a translation of the psychic material must take place...

The concept of *nachtraglichkeit* accentuates the bidirectional arrow of psychic time, such that members live in the present and the past simultaneously. Each session represents "fresh circumstances" in which vertical and horizontal dynamics energize whatever else is taking place. In the clinical incident described below, two contentious participants aired grievances that seem to relate primarily to the here-and-now. The group threatened to become a court of public opinion, as members began adjudicating for a peaceful resolution.

> After four years, Joel felt confident enough in his relationship to the voluble Ellie to call out: "shut up already." Ellie did not take this remark with the warm humor intended. "It's okay for Rich to boss me, but not you." Joel blanched and said little for the session's remainder. He did not appear for the next two weeks, and when I asked him about that he said he was afraid to come back and was thinking of dropping out. "Talk it out with Ellie," I suggested. "No, too afraid to. She's ferocious. Like my mother turning on me."
>
> While Joel first assumed the freedom of a big brother to a younger sister, Ellie's irruption stimulated a traumatic replay of a different family figure: his mother, easily drawn to anger. His father could not restrain her: "I don't think you can protect me from Ellie, not sure that you would even try to." In

contrast, Ellie was the favored child in her household, the only daughter of a household of adoring and protective males, a more beautiful and seductive version of her vociferous mother. She found in me a satisfactory male figure to "boss her," the way she had wished her father could have intervened with her mother.

The two individuals had reexperienced sibling and Oedipal relationships with the intense feelings of their childish mentalities. A fortunate misalliance of inner groupings had occurred. I had no interest in abetting a premature closure or a peaceful resolution but saw no advantage in leaving the underlying dynamics unaddressed. To foster a new "registration," I "translated" some of the earlier developmental epochs that had been superimposed on the present. This led to a discussion of members' varying roles in their originary families and in our group. How did our group "operate" and assign roles and "spokepersons" (Pichon-Rivière, 2017)? Who was my favorite and least favorite child? What roles were feared, wished for, and needed for growth? I silently reviewed my own history with siblings and near-siblings, and the roles I assigned to Ellie and Joel and the roles I could have played.

Bion (1977, pp. 48–49) advised formulating a method that can "penetrate the barrier" between different layers of an analysand's personality, and therefore of different emotional states of mind. By reviewing the "successive epochs" of our own life, the therapist more likely will empathically bridge to others. As a relational process, the group penetrates the core of our identity – we "re-transcribe" and gradually transform along with other members.

Part III

Doing Our Work

Chapter 7

Impasses and Opportunities

In Shakespeare's *Henry IV* (III, 1, 50) Glendower boasts: "I can call spirits from the vasty deeps." Hotspur responds: "Why, so can I, or so can any man; But will they come when you do call for them?" Alas, groups do not happen and run on their own. Leadership is a performative art (Bennis, 2007). We generate, structure, and culture, and monitor a group, and while every group is different, they all bear the imprint of our words. Words matter, and "put it into words" is the implicit and explicit operative. While appreciating the importance of play and nonverbal interactions, we try to place them within the language system.

Yet so often when we speak, our listeners hear only words. Our interventions seem correct and our timing in synch, yet the group is left untouched. To address this situation, we must think more broadly about the nature of human communication, and how we may use ourselves to further a truth-seeking process. Making our task that much more difficult are the brutal realities that no group wants to be yoked to meaning, and everybody lies.

I put forth the notion that truth evasion is universal, as is truth-seeking, and group members, including the therapist, demonstrate both tendencies. At various moments and to varying degrees, group members may pursue conflicting goals regarding the need for psychic truth, pursue different truths, or approach truth differently or not at all. Hence, the *3Rs*, discussed in *Chapter 5*. In this chapter, I describe two complementary models the therapist may use as conceptual tools for pursuing truth. These are Bion's tripartite rubric of the *container-contained*, and my (Billow, 2010c) *four modes of therapeutic discourse* (*diplomacy, integrity, sincerity,* and *authenticity*).

Fixed Patterns of Communication: Narratives, Irruptions, and Polarization

Every social relationship creates itself, with its own culture and implicit rules of engagement and demands for allegiance. Therapists and group members adopt roles that are social and mutually contracted and also represent family roles assumed and assigned to others (Pichon-Rivière, 2017). They allow, but also constrict, the types and range of possible group discourse. "Be real" is often an unstated group message, one that conflicts with numerous messages from past and current locations of social life.

> A member (challenged for "hiding"): "I know, you [members] want me to be real. I hate people who put on an act and I hate doing it by acting nice all the time. It is like all the dinners with my family at a big round table, and we were supposed to tell about our day, but a big act. Couldn't talk about anything real. Not to say that you don't, but I'm not ready."

Being observed, individuals assert control of the data by adopting roles, appearance, and manner, tailoring what the sociologist, Erving Goffman (1959), famously described as a "presentation of the self." Goffman proposed that individuals conspire to act as "teams," stabilizing social settings by preserving certain defining features and conspiring to conceal or play down others. As a group psychotherapy session gets underway, people talk of the weather, favorite restaurants, vacations, current events, and so forth. Discourse may seem trivial, circumstantial, and purely defensive. "Small talk" serves a *phatic* (social) function of establishing a common denominator among members, and it tells us about how they negotiate their social lives. Often, superficialities can be harnessed as metaphors and applied to the dynamics that materialize later.

Still, groups become saturated by *fixed narratives* such as with repetitive and naïve historiographies, fruitless interrogations, and empty self-analyses. People anchor themselves in place and time, shaping experience into stories. And then, they come to tell stories about stories. Locations vary: the "here and there" of extra-group life, the "there and then" of biography, and the "here and now" of replayed group enactments. Inhabiting or narrating established patterns of victimhood, certain members may maintain attitudes of passivity and helplessness, yet also dominate and compete for special recognition (Meissner, 1976).

However, an exception: some deeply traumatized individuals have suffered experiences that are truly "unthinkable" and need to tell and have their narratives witnessed and confirmed. Describing the terrors of Auschwitz, Primo Levi (1996, p. 1) expressed profound self-doubt: "As I sit writing at the table, I myself am not convinced that these things really happened." Traumatized members may communicate in bodily, cognitive, and behavioral disturbances – the all too prevalent manifestations of PTSD (see Leiderman and Buchele, 2025). Group members come to understand such testimonies not by their words alone, but by resonating with the narrator and showing they are moved. In "witnessing" (Billow, 2019b; Grossmark, 2007; Kohon and Perelberg, 2018), the group may succeed in gradually releasing the traumatized individual from overwhelming identifications with his or her story.

Especially in aroused states of perceived threat and confrontation, individuals, groups, and larger social and political organizations tend to resort to *polarized* thinking and behavior. Simplified psychological, moral, and political constructs drive affects, fantasies, and action scenarios. The group therapist must challenge hardening attitudes and antagonisms and contain *irruptive reactions* without being unduly jarring or appearing unempathic.

> A male member referred to his female companion as a "dead fish" that he wanted "to bring back to life." While initially amusing to some of the men, the expression was crude and offensive, and needed to be unpacked, related both to the member's psychology and to his (unconscious) intentions in our group. Did he really expect to be congratulated for the

description of his romantic relationship? What or who was he targeting in our group? But before such questions could be addressed, two female members irrupted in fury, accusing him of seeing females as "frigid," "objects" to be consumed or manipulated. Individuals of both sexes defended the man against their stridency, which only solidified the women's judgments, now extended to the failures of society at large (and by implication, our group).

It seemed clear to me that the session could be deconstructed (*Chapter 7*) to consider a number of themes, including (infantile) omnipotence, sexism, cruelty, dominance, and bully–bullied group enactments (Billow, 2013a). Perhaps representing an aspect of our "animal inheritance" (Bion, 1961), such dynamics seem to play out in all families, groups, and societies.

As a male wanting to introduce a wider perspective, I thought to tread lightly, and I merely commented, "let's stick to our group before we consider society at large." I dreaded what might eventuate in the next session, but the two women came forth immediately, apologizing for what they described as "browbeating." I decided that this was not the time and that I was not the right gender to further explore their antecedent figures and identifications. A more immediate task was to involve the group in acquainting the insight-challenged male with the aggression and condescension in his figurative speech. Not coincidentally, he had taken care of his depressed ("dead") mother and he replayed the helper role in his romantic relationships and in our group. How could he accept that he had anything other than the purist of intentions? In his words: "I'm a lover, not a hater."

Factual Truth, Psychic Truth, and Falsity: Bion's Metapsychological Framework

> In any situation where a thinker is present the thoughts when formulated are expressions of falsities and lies. The only true thought is one that has never found an individual to "contain" it.
>
> (Bion, 1970, p. 117)

A basic tenet of Freud's thought is that pathology is the result of denied truth. Freud (1895) located "proton pseudo," the "first lie," as the heart of hysteria. Unearthing hidden truth provided the road to recovery. Freud first believed secreted truths as veritable but later consigned them to fantasy. He also (Freud 1916/17, p. 336) briefly discussed falsification in relationship to "retrospective phantasying." Lacan (1977, p. 50) had defined the unconscious as "occupied by a falsehood." Bion (1977), however, was unique in placing truth – the need for truth and the need for truth seeking – "*K*" – as the focal point of his metapsychology. He equated emotional awareness with "truth" and mental health. "Lack of such awareness implies a deprivation of truth and truth seems to be essential for psychic health. The effect on the personality of such deprivation is analogous to the effect of physical starvation on the physique" (Bion, 1962, p. 56).

However, Bion concluded that the biological need for the truth strained the limits of our evolution as human beings. "Thinking is embryonic even in the adult and has yet to be developed fully by the race" (Bion, 1962, p. 85). The original function of verbal thought, to provide restraint for motor discharge (Freud, 1911), had to be deflected "to the tasks of self-knowledge for which it is ill-suited and for the purpose of which it has to undergo drastic changes" (Bion, 1962, p. 57).

Bion (1970, p. 9) reserved a special category of evasive response, designated by the Greek letter psi (Ψ), referring to statements "known by the initiator to be false but maintained as a barrier against statements that lead to a psychological upheaval [i.e., growth and change]." Excessive or dramatic presentation of emotion, as well as of words, may represent Ψ, as in the example of rage, "of which the fundamental function is denial of [awareness of] another emotion" (Bion, 1970, p. 20). Given that Bion was not moralizing but speaking about human limitation to tolerate anxiety and pain, I qualify that Ψ may relate to *unconscious* knowing that is refused entry into self-consciousness. Technically, when false statements are offered to provoke, accuse, injure, or to defend oneself unduly, they enter the realms of *-K and -H* (*Chapter 4*).

"Truth" is spelled with a small rather than capital "t." Too often, conventional or familiar ideas are treated as definitive "Truth." In contrast, new or challenging ideas, rather than greeted with interest and curiosity, are ignored or suppressed. Relevant data may be omitted, leaving both speaker and listeners confused or drawing false inferences. And even when factually true, *psi* communications may serve falsity, by being inauthentic, irrelevant, or cliché, so providing a buffer against genuine mental interaction.

In *Experiences*, Bion (1961) described how groups form *basic assumptions*. Members band together to deposit surreptitiously in others or in the group entity itself (via processes of "*projective identification*") their own forbidden wishes, feelings, and fantasies. In his last major book, Bion (1970) supplemented his early work with new formulations. The group, now referred to as the "*Establishment*," is treated as veritable and not primarily as phantasmic. The conflict between truth-seeking and falsity is not conceptualized primarily as intra and interpsychic, but sociopolitical. The *Establishment* seeks to negate anything new and resorts to lying rather than having its ideas disturbed (Bion, 1970, p. 103).

As in *Experiences*, the task of confronting the group with its truth-suppressing tendencies falls to the leader, who Bion (1966, p. 37) exhorts to be an "exceptional individual," or "mystic." The leader functions with "the impact of an explosive force on a preexisting framework," the goal being that the group "should thrive or disintegrate but not be indifferent." Therapeutic relationships foster *ritualization*, and one danger that Bion did not foresee is that we may foist on ourselves, accept, or encourage this heroic persona. A dynamic, evolving group examines and challenges its *Establishment* tendencies, including those promulgated by its leader.

> I was not one of those "uh huh" analysts, the woman acknowledged in the group's discussion of my skills. I spoke my mind and she knew where I stood. I did my job of dealing with every member in a fair-minded, even-handed way. Yet, she protested: "I don't get to see the real you. You wouldn't be like this with your friends and family. This is how therapists are supposed to be."
>
> "Why isn't being like I am with you real, maybe even realer than what passes for social and family life?" I questioned. "I

might have more freedom to be myself here." This led to speculations as to my role as husband and father; some complimentary, others playfully dubious. Several demurred regarding my "even-handedness," some claimed that they didn't always like my "freedom," and some debated who was my "favorite" and why. I no longer felt "exceptional," more like a "real me," and not entirely comfortable.

An aspect of human growth and development is coming to acknowledge and understand, if not fully accept, the self-presentations that each of us feels compelled to adopt to preserve sanity, good spirits, and interpersonal relationships. When uncritically brought to attention, the falsifying aspects of a member's psychology, interpersonal group relationships, or of the group itself, present opportunities for exercising curiosity and furthering discourse. Psychic truths may become more tolerable than hiding from them.

I now describe two complementary models of therapeutic truth seeking: Bion's seminal "*container-contained*" and my "*four strategies of therapeutic discourse*" (Billow, 2009; 2010a; 2010b; 2015). These denote modes of conceptualizing, listening, and speaking as the group cycles through the inevitable processes of *resistance, rebellion*, and *refusal*. The therapist navigates these modes to cement bonding, build trust, reduce falsity, and allow symbolic as well as actual relationships to evolve.

The Three Relational Variations of the Container-Contained

Bion formulated the essential process of how thinking and communicating mutually develop and proceed in terms of a paradigm of "*container-contained*." The model draws attention to how we hear and think about another's communication, how we convey our experience back, and how this communicative interplay impacts the participants and the immediate future of the relationship.

Bion began formulating these ideas in his work with groups. He discovered that a type of countertransference emerged from taking in the members' "*projective identifications*" – characteristics that they projected on to him. Although often painful to absorb and make sense of, the analyst's subjective reactions could be utilized to learn about the group and its members. Bion demonstrated how the clinician, using primary process ("reverie") – the capacity to free-associate, imagine, and dream – and secondary processes, might decipher the patients' projections and draw inferences. The analyst's ensuing transformations (*"containing"*) of the shared experience (the *"contained"*) provided the most reliable basis of interpretations.

As he developed his metapsychology, Bion described processes of symbol formation, human development, internal and external object relations, and learning from (and resisting) emotional experience, all illuminated by the notion of *container-contained*:

> The individual cannot contain the impulses proper to a pair and the pair cannot contain the impulses proper to a group. The psycho-analytic problem is the problem of growth and its harmonious resolution in the relationship between the container and the contained, repeated in individual, pair, and finally group (intra and extra psychically).
> (Bion, 1970, pp. 15–16)

This compressed passage pertains specifically to the inherent problems in human communication and the importance of others in supporting the individual's drive to think and develop meaning. It is a model of emotional learning that develops and is sustained in interaction with others. It describes the workings of productive group process and gives us clarity as to why groups may fail.

Containing is primarily *transformative*, that is, interpretative, even when nonverbal. The group therapist teases out the significance in the ambiguous communications that mark the session. What fantasies, thoughts, and emotions are being conveyed? What is wanted for satisfaction, what is needed legitimately, and what is available realistically? Utilizing primary and secondary processes, the therapist gathers and deciphers the patients' and group's unmediated thoughts and emotions, gradually representing (re-presenting) them in words, gesture, and silence, and when necessary, boundary-maintaining action.

Bion briefly elaborated three variations of the container-contained, which he labelled *symbiotic, commensal*, and *parasitic*. For clarity, I have denoted these prototypes as *bonding, symbolic*, and *anti-linking* relational configurations (Billow, 2000b; 2003).

Bonding

In human development, container-contained processes initially involve *bonding*. Infant–[m]other projective–introjective exchanges establishes crucial emotional and mental links between the infant and the outside world. The infant's symbolic "sojourn in the breast" (Bion, 1962, p. 183) makes manageable the child's need to understand itself and others, placing the need – and its satisfaction – in the relational context. By containing the infant's inchoate feelings, and interesting the infant in them, the receptive [m]other fosters the development of a "normal part" of the infant's personality that concerns itself with psychic quality.

Bonding requires an empathic capacity for what Balint (1968) called "primary love" and Searles (1979) referred to as "therapeutic symbiosis." The receiver must be able to move into and out of states of self-object dedifferentiation to think on the primary-process level of "reverie" (Ogden, 2011), "illusion," "play" (Winnicott, 1971), and "symmetrization" or "homogenization" (Matte-Blanco, 1988; Newirth, 2023). Accommodations may be subtle, communicated by bodily and tonal responses as much as by overt action or actual dialogue, and may be directed toward unexpressed rather than expressed needs.

Bonding communications continue to function as an important source of data collection and responsive interaction in all human relations. Mature dialogue, in which semantic meaning participates fully, rests on the relational bed of such pre-articulate, projective–introjective exchanges. These exchanges are "emotionally rewarding…[establishing] a sense of being in contact…a primitive form of communication that provides a foundation on which, ultimately, verbal communication depends" (Bion, 1967, p. 92).

In *containing*, the therapist accommodates the individual or group's bonding needs, longings, and fears, without mindlessly submitting to or prematurely interpreting them. We differentiate between expressions of genuine needs for contact and regressive enactments, that is between fantasies involved in seeking relatedness and pathologically *entitled* actions merely employed to gratify such wishes. In many instances, the dynamics and behavior of exaggerated *entitlement* may be fruitfully – if not always immediately – interpreted (Billow, 1999b; 1999c; see pp. 100–104 in this volume).

Containing on the *bonding* level may involve limit-setting and other boundary-maintaining procedures, confrontation, verbal reframing, clarification, and interpretation. While the member (or whole group) may not fully understand, or care to understand, the meaning expressed in such interventions, he or she is sensitive to the caring contained in them. Interventions must be delivered and experienced benevolently, their essential purpose being to establish or renew "a sense of contact." When a member refers to my being a "best friend," or "on my side," I think of the early figures with whom they (and I) remain "in contact."

> Rachel had willingly accepted her analyst's invitation to a newly formed group. But several months later, she declared in an individual session her intention to give the group three more sessions before terminating. "I just like individual much better; I get your full attention." In a supervisory consultation, I asked the therapist if he gave Rachel his full attention in group. He had purposefully minimized his involvement with her, "a very attractive young woman." Attending to her would betray his other female patients, as well as unfairly dominate the males. It became apparent that the therapist was anxious not only about giving Rachel special attention, but also about receiving special attention. Showing interest in Rachel would call attention to him too. Other members would monitor and react in unpredictable ways; everyone would be upset by his behavior and would leave group. So Rachel was just one of many who wished to be acknowledged and to directly connect to him. No longer pretending to himself that he was not involved in intimate therapeutic relationships, he found it much easier to look at, talk to, and respond to Rachel.

Notice that it would have been hurtful and inaccurate to interpret Rachel's determination to leave group as a pathologically entitled need for special attention. Indeed, considering the total situation of the transference–countertransference, Rachel's dissatisfaction was a sensitive response to the therapist's withdrawal of bonding established in the individual sessions. Her rebellious threat of secession signalled the analyst to reconsider his group relational gestures.

Group cohesion aggregates from mutual loyalties: the combination of member-to-member, member-to-whole group, and member-to-therapist bonds. While the dynamics of member-therapist bonding may be subtle and unacknowledged, in my opinion they primarily determine the other bonding matrices and the ongoing group process. The entire group monitors and attends to each member's affective bond with the therapist; disruption of a member-to-therapist bond calls attention to itself and becomes a focal point of the work.

Symbolic *Communications*

To an increasing degree, the developing child becomes able to contain feelings while in the [m]other's absence, and to transform perceptions and feelings into rudimentary prototypes of sophisticated thought. In other words, *symbolic thought* now serves the function to develop emotional meaning that was once provided primarily by the other. The child has internalized a model of a thinking couple (the *container-contained*). As *symbolic* links are established with one's own mind and the minds of others, the rudiments of a *psychoanalytic function of the personality* are formed. At this *symbolic* level, members strive to contain the emotional progressions and regressions of being with others and to share one's experience in words.

Anti-linking *Communications*

As we know, psychic development does not proceed smoothly. Thinking and relating may easily regress to the dependent level of bonding or become disrupted. Due to traumatic early failures in caretaker relationships (or in response to severe later traumas), the individual (or the traumatized part of the personality) may experience containing and being contained as untrustworthy, painful, and dangerous. The therapist's *bonding* efforts may be experienced as inauthentic and entrapping, and the individual experiences a good deal of anxiety and little reliable pleasure in empathic contact. The goal of communication becomes to evade, even to destroy, meaning and meaningful emotional exchanges (-*K*). *Anti-linking* communications may be subtle or provocatively direct. Words and actions may seem to be wilfully misinterpreted, stripped of emotional meaning, or turned against the self as well as others.

Negotiating the Relational Variations of the Container-Contained

I condense a sequence of sessions describing my efforts to contain a group of young adolescents referred to as "borderline" or "antisocial." Often, I could only surmise what was occurring in their chaotic lives until informed by an irate parent, high school, or hospital personnel. Some adolescents attended for three or four years or longer. Others left after a short term, while still others had their attendance interrupted by brief incarcerations or stays in out-of-town treatment programs.

> Member 1: "What are you looking at, you dumb, four-eyed bastard." (I wore eyeglasses).
> Member 2: "I was thinking this week, he deserves to be cut up in little pieces and thrown down the toilet."
> Therapist: "What did I do this week?"
> The group (in harmony): "Shut up!"
> "What did he do? He was born."
> "No hatched, in a test-tube."
> "He's one of 'them'."
> "He probably beat his kids."
> "No sex with his wife."
> "He gets drunk as soon as he leaves here—probably, stoned."
> "He's stoned already."

"So am I."

"What a pervert."

"I know he's a pervert."

"You're the pervert." (directed to a member, with admiration)

"We ought to cut off his nuts."

"What nuts? – he's a dickless wonder."

"Get the magnifying glass and the tweezers."

I understood the members to be bonding while also harmlessly evacuating their rage. An admixture of linking and anti-linking maneuvers communicated their need to be reassured that I was not inhuman, unbalanced, or "small." I had to establish in their minds that I was fully equipped to cope with and not be destroyed by, retaliate, or withdraw from their hostile attacks. At some point, I might verbalize with sarcasm my appreciation for the group's interest, profess to be complimented by the preoccupation with my sexual life, such that it was. Or, I might declare: "Same old, same old – boring, very very boring." The group's obscene language and repetitive put-downs threatened to become cliché and utilized to secure an "inoperative" (Pichon-Rivière, 2017), but momentarily exciting field of no-meaning.

But there was incipient meaning, for the group scrutinized my reactions to its treatment of me to assess whether I would replicate, or be different from, the vindictive superego figures of the adolescents' internal and external worlds. During relatively positive and productive phases, the members seemed satisfied that I remained "complimented," that is, unrattled by their hostile volleys, and they proceeded with some success to share important events in their lives. I was "allowed" to participate, even praised for interventions and interpretations which were, in fact, most often simple, but emotionally honest, confrontational, and direct: "Katy comes off tough, but she's a mush inside. A lot of you guys too."

Katy: "That's why he gets my parents' big bucks."

The group shifted back and forth between a "fight–flight" *basic assumption* culture and a rudimentary *workgroup* in which members talked about their lives and could listen to and make symbolic connections. As the bad object of their projections, I was a pervert, eunuch, clown, pariah, villain, evil monster, and so forth. Symbolically, I represented every hated and feared adult. I also represented the "outcast" aspect of each group member. Their lives outside of the office described my life inside it, and I often told them so. On the *symbolic* level of containing, I interpreted their loud flood of obscenity, but on the most important level of *bonding*, I displayed that I was not drowned out by it, and in fact, could enjoy it.

Therapist (with good humor): "Yes, stupid and useless, but not dumb enough not to take your parents' money."

My task was to be a container with firm boundaries which could be traversed, but not violated or destroyed. I had to be alert to, tolerate, and at times challenge the convergence and amplification of primitive emotionality, fantasy, and behavioral potential, represented by the group's split transferences, in which I was both the defiled and longed for object. My genuine affection, as well as availability, regularity, and toleration, although not total acceptance of the members' behaviors, provided the frame in which a verbally-constructive group could cohere. The adolescents could decide (unconsciously as much as consciously) to continue to verbally attack me and the "Establishments" that I represented, or they could work with me. Mostly, they did both.

Importantly, and to varying degrees, the members' use of pathological projective identification, while intensified and amplified in repetitive group enactments, was also *detoxified* by my absorbing as well as interpreting the group's hostility. The group supported emotional development also by giving its members the sense of "connectedness," of belonging and being important, to each other, to me, and to their families that sponsored the treatment. For some of the adolescents, the group served important *bonding* and *symbolizing* functions and became instrumental in their surviving the difficult high school years. Others left satisfied in defeating the experience.

In the face of hostile, *anti-linking* maneuvers, the therapist needs a container for one's own stimulated affects. The therapeutic frame of regulated availability, knowledge and training, and the legitimate *entitlement* to assert limits, all may provide this essential function. By maintaining a nonretaliatory "disrespect" (Caper, 1997) for therapy-destructive behavior, as well as a caring understanding, in time the therapist may disarm *anti-linking* and cultivate longed-for-but-distrusted *bonding* and *symbolic* relatedness.

The three relational variations of the *container-contained* are extremely useful in understanding the shifting and ambiguous realities of human communication. They aid the therapist in the complex task of formulating therapeutic activity that is responsive to the need for meaning at different relational levels. These intersubjective processes evolve in every group (and in every social gathering), as ongoing and shifting self-other evaluations influence decisions to participate at various relational levels.

Four Strategies of Therapeutic Discourse: Diplomacy, Integrity, Sincerity, and Authenticity

"Tell all the truth, but tell it slant," wrote Emily Dickinson (1960, pp. 506–507). "The truth must dazzle gradually, or every man be blind." Therapists "slant" their presentations, varying what truths to examine and those to ignore. To offer protection from too much truth, or too little, we try to balance what others are ready to hear and what we feel is necessary to reveal. We carry forth a twofold task: pursuing emotional truths that are painfully immediate and most meaningful, while shielding truths that are immediate, but too "blinding" to become meaningful. Four strategies are involved.

Diplomacy

Interpersonal relations entail negotiating the not always resolvable divergences of interests and goals, and between what can be known and what is safe to communicate. *Diplomacy* is concerned with establishing and maintaining therapeutic relationships and guarding the security of the members. To some extent, power is shared, albeit unequally, for most often it is the therapist who negotiates among different motivations, affiliations, and beliefs. In being *diplomatic*, leadership is strategic: influencing the group not to express its power in "stereotyped subgroupings" (Agazarian,

1997), scapegoating, or retaliation. *Diplomatic* interventions are not always popular or balanced evenly among all participants.

> Claire, in her early 30s and engaged to be married, recently joined our group but now had second thoughts. "Everyone here has children or is planning to. I don't want any; you're going to think something is wrong with me." Her declaration stirred interest and an incipient interrogation. "This is what I feared, that I would have to explain myself."
>
> I too was interested in exploring the meanings behind Claire's decision, but there was truth in her apprehension that I acknowledged: "Yes, no one would question why one of us would want to have a child. 'Childless' seems to define something negative." Claire felt supported but several of the other women took issue. "I feel you are suppressing me. I just want to learn about Claire." "Should I feel uncomfortable if I talk about being a mother and how wonderful it feels?"
>
> Claire reassured the second speaker that she loved children and enjoyed hearing about them. But she was stung by the accusation of suppression, which she felt was directed to her: "I don't want to suppress you…" and she broke off, near tears but also frozen with anger.
>
> Again, I heard truth in Claire's ostensible misidentification. The first speaker was angry with Claire for her position: announcing yet refusing to explore her decision. There also was justification in the second speaker's anger towards me for making her uncomfortable. I matter-of-factly acknowledged both standpoints, neither of which seemed untenable. Claire was not willing to have a child or to talk about it at this time. She had declared her turf, and I secured her right to it. Apparently I had made others angry at me too. My summary statement served its purpose of cooling the situation sufficiently, and the session proceeded with relatively peaceful co-existence.
>
> The strategy behind my assertion of power and authority was to forestall an open confrontation between a prematurely interpreting group and a member who would secede rather than abdicate a position of refusal (*Chapter 4*). At this stage

of initiation of the new member, it was important to identify the mutual hostility but not encourage a "gang up" of group exploration. I deflected some of the anger to a safer target: me.

Integrity

Integrity would seem to present little ambiguity since the therapist can rely on a clear set of moral and ethical conventions. However, integrity emerges not only from principles, but also how and where they are applied. As the "Mayfair Madam," Sydney Biddle Barrows (1986) acknowledged "I ran the wrong kind of business [prostitution], but I did it with integrity." Samuel Johnson clarified that "integrity without knowledge is weak and useless, and knowledge without integrity is dangerous and dreadful." For the clinician, *self*-knowledge is important; it is the lens through which to evaluate moral truth and falsity in the group and in the members' narrations.

> Scott occupied many group sessions vilifying his wife, who had been, and possibly continued to be, unfaithful. Now he reported an incident in which his wife, tussling with their adolescent daughter over control of the television remote control, left a bite mark on her arm. The next day, the therapist telephoned and requested that Scott appear immediately in her office. She explained: "I was troubled all night by what I heard, and I think I might be required to call Child Protective Service to report abuse."
>
> Scott (enraged): "My wife and daughter have a great relationship! You know that! She's not an abusive mother. You must hate her as much as I do!" He stormed out of the office: "I don't think I can come back to the group."
>
> Although mostly secretive about group, Scott shared this incident with his wife, who responded sympathetically. At the same time, she empathized with the therapist: "I'm sure I don't have the best reputation with her" and encouraged him to return to group and attempt to work it out. This did not entirely please the husband, who, while mollified towards the therapist, now had to present a different view of his wife to his

group. For, even when hearing falsities about herself as an unfit mother, she had remained steadfast, empathic to her accuser, and loyal to her husband and his need for therapy. To reconciliate with the wife – and with the group – all would have to inspect Scott's "truth" and how he misused it in narrating a one-sided view of his wife.

Cohen and Schermer (2002) described the "moral order" of a group, referring to its norms, values, beliefs, and ambience, and which supplies a context for each member's group self and the group's collective conscience and ego ideal. In my view, the leader personifies this ideal and without reflection, may take on a moral mantle. Rulebooks are ever-present, symbolic, but also real. They guide but also may mislead. There are multiple "rights" and "wrongs" and not all of them are acknowledged in a member's narration. Our urges for fairness and "equal treatment for all" must include consideration of those who are not present but sanctified or vilified.

Sincerity

Sincerity conveys felt feeling and conscious intention. "One cannot both be sincere and seem so," Andre Gide averred. *Sincerity* is categorical – either you are or not. *Sincerity* is always simple, and sometimes simplistic. As Oscar Wilde cautioned: "All bad poetry springs from genuine feeling" (in Trilling, 1972, p. 119). Mere consciousnesses of positive or negative feelings and expressing them publicly does not automatically advance relationships. No matter how sincere our feelings and intentions are, we cannot be fully aware or certain of our motivations, meanings, or interpersonal consequences.

> An analyst had established a warm relationship with Helene, a patient in combined treatment. Helene had endured several miscarriages and, nearing 40 years old, she feared becoming infertile. Being the trusted witness to Helene's travails, the therapist felt increasingly uncomfortable withholding her own parallel experience. At a moment that she felt it beneficial, the

therapist disclosed that she also had married in her late 30s and described similar difficulties in childbearing. Helene seemed reassured when the therapist revealed that she was the mother of two thriving teenagers.

Now, pregnant again and halfway to full term, Helene came into a group session announcing that the fetus had died, and she would have to have an abortion. The therapist cried along with the patient, which touched the members, who concurred that the therapist "really cared." Was she crying for Helene or for her earlier self? the therapist wondered. She felt herself to be false, undeserving of the credit for "caring," since the group did not know of her own reproductive struggles and identification with Helene. And, in her atypical display of emotion, the therapist was concerned that she drew attention to herself, depriving the anguished Helene.

The patient had a different take; much later, Helene revealed apologetically that, if she could not deliver a healthy child, she would be a disappointment to the therapist.

Authenticity

Whereas *sincerity* is categorical and simple, *authenticity* is dynamic and complex: tension exists between self-awareness and expression. Communications are mediated by appreciation of the dimensionality of emotion, the influence of the irrational and unconscious, and the inescapability of social role. In his monograph, *Sincerity and Authenticity*, Lionel Trilling (1972, p. 11) emphasized how *authenticity* involves "a more strenuous moral experience than 'sincerity' does, a more exigent conception of the self and of what being true to it consists of a wider reference to the universe and man's place in it, and a less acceptant and genial view of the social circumstances of life."

In my conceptualization, *sincerity* derives from the dynamics of idealization and devaluation, characteristic of paranoid-schizoid or "manic" mental states. Splitting remains prominent as a mode of organizing experience (good/bad; exciting/boring, etc.). In contrast, *authenticity* signifies the hallmark of the depressive position: the capacity to experience ambivalent feelings while maintaining a balanced and humane outlook. Uncongenial circumstances of social life inevitably get stimulated by group and must become part of a "less acceptant" but more *authentic* experience. *Authenticity* also requires mental and sometimes behavioral efforts to repair the harm we have caused, both imagined and real.

> The usually compliant Seth summoned courage to report that he had felt "ambushed" when I began the new year with the announcement of a raise in group fee. "I have no choice [in your decision]," Seth protested. "It would be fairer if you had discussed it first in group." Other members disagreed: "This is what other doctors do." "It wouldn't make a difference; he does what he wants." "It's Richard's right to set the fee." "We don't have to stay."
>
> In speaking up forcibly, Seth became less "genial" and "acceptant." He had made a fair point and, despite my support from other group members, I felt embarrassed, and remorse for hurting. But I was also annoyed, as if Seth was ungrateful for making so much of the issue. After all, I was entitled to raise my rates, which were not exorbitant, and he was benefiting from my efforts. I had to tolerate the mix of pleasant and unpleasant feelings towards Seth and support his efforts at being authentic (as well as my own). I said that I had not realized that he had felt ambushed, and that I would do as he suggested next time, even if no one else seems to care. Seth was delighted: "I didn't expect to be heard." My reparative gesture, both spontaneous and deliberate, only partially relieved the exaggerated guilt I felt for "damaging" him.

Entitlement to Lead

I conclude this chapter by addressing the therapist's evaluation of and use of *entitlement*: the assertion of power and privilege. "Every profound spirit needs a mask," Nietzsche asserted (Trilling, 1972, p. 119). Therapists and members wear masks that allow individuals to relate to each other in ways not otherwise possible. These roles are defined by the therapist and not mutually contracted, however. All members are "little nodal points" in the social network of group (Foulkes, 1964, p. 292), but not all of one size and shape. The therapist's entitlements bring power, control, and directionality to the group, which privileges and prohibits modes of interactions (see McLaughlin, 1991).

The dyadic therapist "both metaphorically and actually sits in the most comfortable seat, controls the time and place of meeting, receives payment, and is protected from discomfort" (Michels, 1988, p. 55). The group therapist, in contrast, is less protected and must deal with the members' mixed reactions to one's leadership (the *3Rs*). In either modality, the therapeutic frame may be perceived as a "recreation of childhood experiences in which one's own rights and entitlements were subordinated to those of others (Michels, 1988, p. 55). Dynamics of *legitimate, exaggerated*, or *inhibited entitlement* belong to us as well as to other members. As Freud (1916, p. 315) candidly acknowledged, each of us harbors irrational entitlement: "We all demand reparation for early wounds to our narcissism, our self-love." My viewpoint varies from the tradition that considers entitlement primarily as an aspect of a patient's pathological narcissism while neglecting therapist and interactional dynamics (Billow, 1997; 1999a; 1999b).

Blechner (1987) characterized two strategies for treating entitlement: "frustration" and "gratification." I prefer the verbs "interpretating" and "accommodating." The first, originally promulgated by Freud (1916), emphasizes maintaining traditional psychoanalytic boundaries and recommends analyzing dynamic, genetic roots of disturbances in healthy entitlement. Michels (1988, p. 56) advised not "to placate or mollify the patient by gratifications that grow out of a desire to dilute the patient's resentment and disappointment or bribe him into pseudo compliance...the therapist must be sensitized to...accepting and tolerating anger or dissatisfaction and interpreting resistances to expressing, or even experiencing, the frustrations of the treatment."

Winnicott and Kohut, in contrast, viewed disturbed entitlements as expressions of need, and they attempted to adapt the environment so that the patients may experience the underlying desired, aims, and objects. Therapists influenced by their theories have stressed the importance, and often the inevitability, of living through a lengthy period in which the therapist provides a holding environment before the patient or member is ready to tolerate interpretative activity. So as not to "forfeit" a trust-building stage of healthy entitlement, the therapist must distinguish a period of "normal and necessary omnipotence (specialness, uniqueness) from pathological omnipotence" (Grotstein, 1995, p. 6). At times, as in *containing* at the level of *bonding*, manifest wishes are therapeutically gratified without analysis.

> "How are you contributing to the group?" I asked Randy (a long-standing member), cutting short his recount of an ongoing struggle with his wife involving his uncooperating with household tasks.
> "Maybe they [other members] can relate to their issues," Randy offered unconvincingly. Another man rejoined sarcastically: "It doesn't relate to me, I take out the garbage and don't have to be asked."
> Ignoring the group's resonant mockery, Randy continued. I interrupted again: "Randy, you're making yourself the butt of the group, it's not good for you, or for the group. Isn't this what you do in your marriage?"
> Randy launched once more into a defence of his marital behavior, and I said he had to stop and respect my leadership. "But no one else is complaining, Rich. You're making me angry." I responded: "I understand that, but you'll have to control yourself and give other people a chance to talk." Randy replied with a disgusted sigh: "I can't understand why you would say that! You're supposed to be a sympathetic professional."
> Randy gave up the floor, but shortly interjected: "You don't talk the same way to other people." "I don't have to," I countered. Randy: "All you care about is your group, the big bucks." "Not 'all', but some," I acknowledged, "I care about the group and I care about supporting myself, now let's move on."

I have discovered that when addressing entitlement, individuals often are more than willing to turn attention from themselves to their therapist, whose techniques and personality may become a focus of discomforting group scrutiny. In addition to projecting, they often make accurate forays into our use and abuse of therapeutic entitlements. Randy implicitly adhered to the accommodation or gratifying theory of therapy in which he considered his repetitive airing of resentments to be a right, and, a method of cure. He found me to be unsympathetic in even introducing the frustration-interpreting theory. Despite his tendencies to *anti-linking*, he had named a truth about my entitlement. I was *supposed* to be *sincere*, a sympathetic professional, but other feelings predominated, including my wish to follow my approach rather than his. My primary motivation was to "govern" the group system *diplomatically* and with *integrity*. However, to be *authentic*, I had to acknowledge that my motivations were also self-serving, expressing my values and to some extent satisfying my own aesthetic, emotional, intellectual, and fiscal needs.

In practice, each clinician finds his or her own compromise between gratification and frustration, accommodation and interpretation. But on what basis is the compromise reached? How do we know when a member is ready to move on and can tolerate the frustration of non-accommodation? There is, of course, no definitive or purely objective method of assessment. Going along with insistent narratives and enactments may represent an escape from "exigencies" of authentic work. On the other end of the interpretation–accommodation continuum, the therapist may precipitously intrude upon a member's psychic readiness, taking an opportunity that does not exist. Randy brought me to my "entitlement threshold," and I could not be sure if and when my retaliatory counter-entitlements came into play.

According to Modell (1976, p. 494), the analyst implicitly must possess "some powerful qualities so that change may be affected merely by being in his presence." However, no therapist feels powerful consistently. I carry with me a feeling of powerlessness, even when I also feel powerful. Members may feel powerless, but we know that patients share power in any ongoing treatment relationship. A stubbornly inhibited or unrevealing group member may control the flow of the session as much as an insistent member such as Randy. Each group session reveals implicit or explicit power struggles among all participants. In doing our work, we vary in our feelings of entitlement and may inhibit or exaggerate its use. For all individuals, attitudes of entitlement are never completely normalized and constructive entitlement is never permanently sustained. When the therapist becomes aware and addresses entitlements – "mine and yours" – benefits may accrue for all participants (Billow, 2019c).

Chapter 8

The Group as a Psychoanalytic Object

Bion (1961, p. 143) asserted that "every group however casual meets to 'do' something," and that well-functioning groups share a "common purpose." More precisely, individuals come together with different constructive purposes in mind, although they share many goals, such as wanting to feel better, get closer to people, resolve ambivalence and confusion, and solve problems. Our work is not only about such common purposes but also involves a curative motive, described with many metaphors: "move the needle," "push the envelope," "break through," and "transform." We strive to do something that is uncommon: to convert a group into a gathering of *psychoanalytic objects*.

Bion (1963) briefly introduced the concept of the *psychoanalytic object* in the context of dyadic treatment. He conceptualized the *psychanalytic object* as emerging from the analysand's discourse and behavior and brought to interpretative meaning by the analyst, who uses observation, theory, emotional experience, and intuition. A *psychoanalytic object* exists not as a tangible object, but as an *idea* that could provide a conceptual (psychoanalytic) framework to view events through a common interpretive lens. This involves treating others and ourselves both as tangible beings and as representatives/transmitters of varying *emotional ideas*, and hence, as *psychoanalytic objects*. I try to convey this point of view when I say to a member (with some irony): "Don't take X's comments to you so personally, they are about him, even if directed to you. *You* have to decide how they apply." Of course, we take what is said to us personally, but to participate in a psychoanalytic

DOI: 10.4324/9781032703251-11

enterprise, we accept that all reflections are also *self-reflections*, and that they represent what Bion referred to as *"opinions."* At best, opinions convey emotional truths, but they are not facts. What is "common" among group members who are thinking psychoanalytically is the willingness to offer and consider *emotional thoughts*; these represent second opinions, and third, fourth, etc.

Psychoanalytic Objects and Nuclear Ideas

Bion's concept propelled my formulation of the *"nuclear idea"* (Billow, 2015). While Bion narrowly characterized the *psychoanalytic object* as arising from the analyst's attention, I stress that a *nuclear idea* may arise from member sources as well, although they are most often brought to focus by the therapist's maintaining the frame of psychoanalytic thinking. As with a *psychoanalytic object*, the *nuclear idea* may focus initially on a personality, such as a member, the therapist, an originary or current figure, a personality trait or dimension of psychology, or any idea that could be a topic of group attention and foster symbolic thinking.

Nuclear ideas emerge from the nucleus of the group process – not only from the therapist's mind. They arise from intersubjective forces and locations that cannot be fully specified, yet may be possible to observe, name, and utilize clinically. Monologues, dialogues, subgroup and group interchanges, feelings, beliefs, memories, "free-associations," enactments, and so forth, all generate the potential to produce a generative *nuclear idea*. Something has transpired – an existential and intersubjective moment or sequence of moments has been or could be partially articulated in words or behavior. Foulkes and Anthony (1965, p. 151) referred to a similar group process as *"condensation,"* an unexpected coalescence of shared meaning involving "an accumulative activation at the deepest levels." The therapist may take the opportunity to conceptualize further and negotiate meaning with member co-participation.

Developing the *nuclear idea* provides a framework for how the therapist – and the group itself – establishes and maintains *coherence* (Pines, 2010). Groups organize themselves – with the therapist's participation and influence – by developing *nuclear ideas*.

They are vehicles through which members individually and collectively come to reflect psychoanalytically.

"I'm just letting everyone know that I'm going to miss the next couple of weeks," said a member of four years. He was surprised when people inquired as to his plans. I was surprised by his surprise and asked him: "Why are you surprised?" Another member joined: "I don't expect people to be interested in me when I'm not here. But I'm interested in you [the other members]." "I'm not surprised, I feel the same way, I will miss you, but I know I'm not missed," echoed several others.

I found this curious, given that people regularly began with "Where's so and so?" "How's so and so?" Absences were noted and talked about. In individual sessions, group cohorts recurrently referred to and inquired and worried about other members. "Everyone seems to miss everyone else, but nobody feels they're missed," I summarized. Several members initially dissented, but they re-examined their feelings in the interlude that followed: "I never felt that my parents were truly excited to see me." "My father practiced 'children should be seen and not heard.'" "I don't know why my parents had children, we seemed to be ignored." "My sister was the pretty one; I was supposed to be smart, and if I wasn't saying something that grabbed their [the family's} interest, forget about it, I mean, forget me." "It was about my mother, never about us."

Members acknowledged furtively registering greeting and departing rituals: how and if they were addressed in the waiting room and who said good-bye and to whom. Only some members anticipated a friendly reception at the start of the session. Group etiquette included "taking turns," monitoring frequency and duration of "talking about oneself," and "attempting to interest others, but never being sure." Post-session fears included retributive "freeze outs" for inadvertently hurting others by expressing their opinions. From one member: "I hear my mother saying, 'I'm not talking to you until you apologize.' She could go on ignoring me for weeks." "My father told me to leave the house until I got a haircut. I just returned early to college instead. He never reached out, I had to do that eventually." "Mine stopped talking to me for six months and I don't remember why."

I had stumbled upon a group mythos – a belief shared by most members, which was captured by the nuclear idea: "Everyone seems to miss everyone else, but nobody feels they're missed." The nuclear idea provided an opportunity to assess and publicize the depth of the commitment to an emotional belief that I had been ignorant of and had surprised me. My words were spontaneous and ironic, perhaps obvious, yet they captured an important and unexamined emotional truth. Here was a group where each member testified to the value of the others. Reiterating the sense of not feeling missed in the face of contrary data made vivid the power of trauma and the difficulty of modifying or eradicating its effects on how we think and what we think about.

Not mentioned in our discussion, but perhaps universal, is the harsh reality of not being missed. Not only Oedipus or those traumatically neglected or abused but the child in each of us deals with the ungraspable facts of not being wanted for oneself and not missed. As parents once claimed their sexual relationship, our loved ones claim their private spaces. And too, a future looms wherein we – like many long-departed group members – will not be remembered.

A nuclear idea is more than merely a *theme*, which can usually be summed up in a single sentence and is unidimensional. A nuclear idea functions on many dimensions: conscious, intrapsychic, relational, existential, and so forth. Nuclear ideas possess psychoanalytic depth, relevant to the individual and to the group's psychodynamics. They are not just focused on the here-and-now, nor to be explored exclusively on that group process level. The nuclear idea (a) gives opportunity for new meaning and depth to any experience that has occurred before or is ongoing in intrapsychic and group relations; (b) focuses participants' attention and provides a mode of entry; (c) establishes a shared activity and common goal of understanding; (d) privileges group members as potential sources of transformation; (e) conveys a sense of order to and mutual appreciation of the group; and (f) creates interest in and valorizes attending to other *nuclear ideas*, such that psychoanalytic metapsychologizing becomes part of group culture and process. Developing *nuclear ideas* circumvents (and may even anticipate) the type of meaning deprivation that leads to a profusion of exaggerated *basic assumptions, common tensions* (Ezriel, 1950), and *focal conflicts* (Whitaker, 1989), and which encourages static *resistances* and unproductive *rebellions* and *refusals*.

Sense, Myth, and Passion

Bion (1963) referred to three integrated qualities of a *psychoanalytic object* as, respectively, *sense, myth*, and *passion*. I have decoded Bion's poetic formulations to make them more comprehensible.

Sense

The experiential dimension of *sense* provides empirical and communicable reference. As in the above example about not being missed, *sense* is established not only by what people say, but *how* they are communicating: their affects, emphasis, and behavioral and paraverbal signaling, such as sighs, conspiratorial glances, laughter, tears, outcries, or sudden silence.

Myth

Myth refers to underlying *symbolic meanings* embedded in group discourse and enactments. They provide access to intergenerationally transmitted "*enigmatic messages*" (Laplanche, 1999). These are the conflicting and often unshakable emotional ideas and impulses that lie at the foundation of one's psychology and often exist without awareness. Myths create a frame for personal identity, ethnicity, cultural value, and the roles members play and have played in families and social organizations, which now includes the group. The members transported a shared (and perhaps universal) *myth* of not being missed to each session's here-and-now.

Passion

Bion (1963, pp. 12–13) defined *passion* ambiguously and not in complete correspondence with its commonplace meaning: "the component derived from L, H, and K. I mean the term to represent an emotion experienced with intensity and warmth though without any suggestion of violence." Etymologically, passion draws on its Latin derivation, meaning suffering or submission. In the example above, the members suffered the emotional realizations accompanying the *nuclear idea* of not being missed and submitted to their painful feelings and thoughts. Overt displays of affects, as in confrontation, ventilation, or abreaction, are not the essence or evidence of *passion*, and group process without passion may seem lively or lifeless. Passionate groups use language in different ways and at different moments to represent *LHK*.

> One group frequently uses exaggerated verbal communication and tone, as in "I'd like to strangle you right now, you're so stubborn;" or "should we stop obsessing about our relationship and just have sex. Isn't that what's going on?" The group's provocative language evokes thought and contributes to the evolution and expansion of consciousness (and unconsciousness) of emotional meaning. In another group, not any less passionate, similar words would be considered violent and frightening. This group maintains the more conventional vocabulary of *LHK*: "I really didn't like it when you..." (+H); or "I was wondering about sexual feelings..." (+KL), and so forth.

Passion involves being receptive to the derivatives of our basic emotions, the primal affects involving loving, hating, and curiosity (*LHK*+/-), as we link our own mind to the minds of others. A suitable term to describe the metapsychology of psychoanalytic *passion* is "primary reception." A thinking mind is available to greet "opinions" freshly. One has achieved the mental clarity and moral freedom (Racker, 1968) to feel, if not say, whatever comes to mind. While *passion* does not compel a particular style of group membership or leadership, it does require establishing the group as the place to think about *psychoanalytic objects* and form *nuclear ideas.*

Deconstructive–Reconstructive Group Process

In order to preserve a well-working group, or attend to the difficulties of an ineffective one, the analytically inclined therapist wears two faces: being constructive and *deconstructive*. To aid the group in reconsidering familiar narratives, to expand categories of thinking and being, and to give voice to the disempowered, we disturb the very status quo that we work to establish. We contest characterological boundaries, falsities, prejudices, prejudgments, and collusions that obstruct or preclude emotional learning. When we say, "stay in the room," redirect attention to a disregarded or unnoticed interaction, play with words and metaphors, or even raise a quizzical eyebrow, we are making a *deconstructive intervention*. We set out to dismantle a conventional mental set to stimulate emotional thinking and relational potentialities. In contrast to an emphasis on here-and-now interactions and rapid shifts of attention from one member to another, the deconstructive–reconstructive process needs time and reflective space.

Freud: Our Premier Deconstructionist

Along with other great late 19th-century and 20th-century thinkers, Freud was a prominent forerunner of deconstruction: "I was one of those who have 'disturbed the sleep of the world'" (Freud, 1914, p. 21). We are following Freud when we "stir up contradiction" (1914, p. 8), imputing alternative or diverse motivation and meaning to clinical discourse and enactments. Psychoanalysis may be conceived of as a series of deconstructions of Freud's work. Many of his ideas, diagnostic formulations, and methods have been modified (such as drive theory, frequency of sessions, and use of the couch), rejected (the "death instinct"), supplemented (child analysis and group treatment), or reformulated with different emphasis (e.g., ego psychology, object relations, interpersonal, and self-psychology). Nonetheless, despite proclamations and emendations, many of Freud's ideas, principles, and procedures remain intact, such as privileging unconscious influence, scrutinizing interactional patterns of the therapeutic participants, examining familial and sociocultural influence, and relying on a "talking cure."

So, while brought to the vernacular by the writings of its founder, Jacques Derrida (2005), deconstructionism existed before Deconstructionism. Parents are our first deconstructionists, as they introduce novelty and surprise, and gently tease and defy cognitive expectations. Parent–child interplay expands the infant's range of thinking and potential meaning, and respects diversity by empowering the infant's perspective. Derrida insisted that deconstruction was part of a living dialogue rather than a superimposed method. Still, *deconstruction* utilizes specific rhetorical skills, serves specific therapeutic purposes, and works in conjunction with developing the *psychoanalytic function of the personality*.

> Ben reported missing the last session because he had ear trouble. "It's related to TMJ – jaw locking. I get it when I feel anxiety that something bad is going to happen and it is my fault. I'm trying to become aware when I feel that way, before I start clenching."
>
> Anna: "Listening to your pain makes me want to reach out and give you a hug and say, are you okay?"
>
> Ben: "I try to focus on where my bad feelings are coming from – why do feel this way about myself? – and sometimes that helps me relax my jaw."
>
> Another member: "When I get self-critical, my back tenses."
>
> Several rapidly picked up the theme of being self-critical and offered their methods of self-cure, such as practicing "forgiveness" or meditating. At one point, I interrupted the process (addressing Ben): "You seemed to have difficulty relaxing into Anna's hug. [Ironically to the group] Everyone seems 'clenched up;' no one seems very relaxed right now."
>
> Members (to Ben): "You moved away from Anna and got intellectual." "And then we all did." "We 'locked up' ourselves."
>
> Anna: "I'm a hugger, but I thought maybe Ben isn't, and that I went too far. I became self-critical about what I said. That's how I 'clench.'"
>
> Ben's preoccupations and obsessive defences had spread to the whole group. In juxtaposing "locked" and "relaxed" I implicated what was not happening, but that could happen if members would "unlock" and "embrace" their emotional

experience. Deconstructing "TMJ" from its literal context and treating it metaphorically encouraged members to reflect playfully and less self-critically on their self-critical behavior, which had become an unstated nuclear idea.

The British philosopher of linguistics, Paul Grice (1989) had introduced the technical term "*implicate*" to describe certain types of indirect "speech acts" essential to deconstruction. These rhetorical devices include metaphor, humor, sarcasm and irony, exaggeration, understatement ("lititotes"), intonation, and emphasis. In calling attention to multiple and contradictory meanings and motivations that might be directing the group, the therapist's deconstructive speech acts attune members to the nuances of self-presentation, to distinguish what is said from what might be implied or suggested.

Shakespeare's *Julius Caesar* provides a dramatic example of *implication*. Mark Anthony's "Brutus is an honourable man" deconstructed a truth claim ("honourable") by contrasting it with an unstated antonym ("dishonourable"). Anthony's deconstructive rhetoric swayed the group of Roman senators and citizens to switch allegiances and take up arms. What happens to the group's narratives when the therapist deconstructs? Repeating words with an ironic tone, or a different emphasis, grafts a different, alternative, or expanded representation. Deconstructions invite the development of *nuclear ideas.*

Lacan insisted that if psychoanalytic work is to be effective, it must shatter the mirror erected to define oneself, an ego-image that shields the self from the reality of the Other (the Real). "As in a silvered mirror—if you look carefully, there isn't just one image, but a second one, which splits, and if the silver is thick enough, there are ten, twenty, an infinity" (Lacan, 1978, p. 269). Using the same image, Foulkes (1964, p. 110) analogized the group as a "hall of mirrors," wherein "a person sees himself, or part of himself—often repressed part of himself—reflected in the interactions of other group members. He also gets to know himself…by the effect he has upon and the picture they form of him." Deconstructions shatter halls-of-mirrors: the static narratives and intellectualized self-other reflections and entrap a group within. They introduce more complex relational views.

Betina, approaching 40, explained her unhappy single status as not yet having found "the right one." When members gently questioned what she meant by the term and what she was looking for, she teared up. "I feel you are blaming me." The group had attempted to examine her assumptions, words, and actions, but her tears had shut them down. So I continued. Aware that she had blamed the group for blaming her, I could easily blame her for that and monitored my ironic rhetoric.

Therapist: "What is so bad about accepting blame?"
Betina: "It makes me feel like a bad person."
Therapist: "Well, how bad are you?"
Betina: "It hurts to be criticized."
Therapist: "You don't want helpful criticism either?"
Betina: "Just praise" (with a self-aware smile).

So often, our interventions may be challenged as not being the "right ones," but who's to judge? The member's conscious or unconscious? The group itself? You? Me? I felt I had a choice: leaving the individual in her own solipsistic world or deconstructing it.

A number of words and terms were re-examined in this interaction and left open for further reflection, the truth values uncertain: "right one"; "blame"; "bad person"; "bad"; and "criticism." To deconstruct others, the therapist must make efforts to deconstruct facile leadership. Who we are, what we say, and how we say it (and remain silent) influence the group's deconstructive process.

A caveat. Winnicott (1971) insisted on the importance of verbal play in adult treatment, as it manifests in the therapist's choice of words, inflections of voice, and sense of humor. However, not everyone shares our sense of humor, or benefits from the full array of communicative strategies. A member or the group may not understand the intended meaning of a deconstructive intervention or its goals. To open things up emotionally and provide mental space for deconstruction, therapists also nail down discourse. We clarify, interpret, and even offer definitive answers to resolve unnecessary confusions or end fruitless debates. Some individuals, entering with narrow conceptual and emotional boundaries, offer fewer communicative options than those with emotional flexibility and a well-developed capacity for symbolic play. Our goal is to challenge certain thoughts without attacking the thinker or the group itself. When we deconstruct, we want to make sure that things come together again.

Loving Our Work

Freud (1921, p. 92) reasoned that "a group is clearly held together by a power of some kind: and to what power could this feat be better ascribed than Eros, which holds together everything in the world." He described psychoanalysis as "in essence a cure through love" (Freud and Jung, 1974, pp. 12–13), although he was referring to the patient's relationship to the doctor and not a process of mutuality. "In so far as his [patient's] transference bears a 'plus' sign, it clothes the doctor with authority and is transformed into belief in his communications and explanations" (Freud, 1916/17, p. 445). The therapist must also function in the realm of "plus." Bach (2006, pp. 129–130) argued that to do productive work, the therapist must come to know, appreciate, and admire analytic co-participants "in essentially the same way one appreciates the body and flesh of one's closest friends or one's own children in their entirely." I am alerted to possible trauma in a member's life when I cannot find evidence of "plus" in myself, when it becomes intense, arousing, or disquieting, or when I feel defensive about it.

Bion (1965, p. 70) reasoned that "an L relationship clearly cannot be regarded as excluding K either in logic or reality." Racker (1968, p.174) asserted similarly: "to understand, to unite with another, and hence, also to love, prove to be basically one and the same." In the group context, Foulkes and Anthony (1965) termed the "supportive" factor, and Scheidlinger (1964) the "experiential," both referring to the therapist's fostering a climate of permissiveness, acceptance, and belonging. Yalom (1995, p. 106) stressed that "underlying all consideration of technique must be a consistent, positive relationship between therapist and patient. The basic posture of the therapist to a patient must be one of concern, acceptance, genuineness, empathy." However, this therapeutic posture, Yalom clarified, does not preclude confronting the patient, showing irritation and frustration, or even suggesting that an individual consider leaving the group. A loving analytic attitude finds expression in manner, tone, and nonverbal signs of emotional engagement. Particularly when expressing hate (Winnicott, 1949), interventions need to be offered with benevolence.

Still, even today, therapists are often more uncomfortable with their patients' expressions of positive feelings, such as sexuality, love, and dependency, than with negative feelings, and make tacit agreements with patients to avoid them (Jacobs, 2001). Our insights may rightly be valued for their effort and concern as much as for their acuity and depth. "The truth rebels," Lacan (1967/2002, p. 267) consoles us, "however inexact it might be one has all the same tickled something." We need to tickle and be tickled too – capable and *willing* to approach interactions with an unwavering loving attitude to help individuals – oneself included – claim potentials. For me, this is the core of being relational: encouraging loving interest in the mind and body of others and ourselves.

> Irma casually mentioned a "private" session in which another member, John, had been discussed. A relatively new member, Max, broke in (agitated): "I have my doubts about you, Rich. You talk about your individual sessions with other patients." I waited, nonverbally encouraging him, or others, to say more about this possibility. Only Max continued, shifting the ostensible topic of grievance. "Your policy of charging for missed sessions. I wonder if you have different rates for different patients."
>
> Group members (protesting): "What if he did?" "Why does it bother you?" "Maybe it isn't all about the money – the way it is for you."
>
> Irma (to me): "I feel so bad for getting you in trouble. (to Max) "Rich didn't say anything. I just knew that he knew what I was saying about John and agreed."
>
> I reassured Irma: "I'm not in trouble. You don't have to explain." Several members – including John – expressed confidence in my keeping confidentiality. Now a fourth member, Carl, burst out angrily to Max: "If you can't trust your therapist, you should go somewhere else. You need to own what you're doing, and not lay it on Rich."

Max, unperturbed, returned to me: "I know this is my issue too. I don't trust people, and my wife doesn't trust me, and for good reason. But when I asked you in individual about charging people different rates you said you wouldn't answer until the end of the session so that I could explore what I was feeling – I thought that was patronizing, but helpful."

I again received support: "What's wrong with what he said?" "Why is that patronizing?" "Rich can never win with you."

"Don't listen to them," I advised Max, with a conspiratorial smile. "They are a bunch of puppies. 'Yip yip yip.'"

Max (only slightly amused): "They protect you, all the time. And you don't need protection."

"Maybe they love me."

Max (softening): "They do…I loved my last therapist."

"Could you love me?"

Max: "It's a distinct possibility. But I wouldn't trust you. This is all from my mother, I know that. She said not to trust anybody."

"But you trusted her to take her advice, and you trust me enough to say you don't trust me."

Max: "Yeah, she would have killed me if I challenged her."

Therapist: "Well, you did it pretty good. No pot shots – you seemed to be careful not to purposely hurt me."

Max blushed, and when the group pursued what he was feeling, he smiled sheepishly and brushed aside their efforts. "A small step for humanity, but a giant leap for Max," I offered. The group laughed.

Max flashed me an appreciative smile: "Thank you, you got me off the hook." A faint flush reappeared before he turned away.

The group had expressed anger about how Max spoke to me and criticized my work, and apparently, they needed to review. "It must have been difficult when your integrity is challenged." "I would have felt humiliated." "I would have told him to go fuck himself." "I still feel guilty when accused, even if I know I didn't do anything wrong. And then I get pissed." "I can feel guilty when anyone is accused! I am a bad person and must be responsible. I usually don't say anything."

I responded: "At one time, for sure. All of what you are describing. Now I think about why someone would want to put me down – maybe I did something too. No one likes paying for missed sessions. [to Max] You took a chance with all of us, not only with me."

I had to protect the group process from my protectors, Irma, John, perhaps the whole group, and moralizers, such as Carl, who instructed Max to "own" his behavior. In modifying his more typical unreflective antagonism in our exchanges, Max had begun to do just that. My ironic humor supported Max's claim – which he himself only partially believed, that his compliant group cohorts – "a bunch of puppies" – like their leader, could not be trusted. "Canine words" ("yip yip yip") conveyed a reassuring "tickling" signal to the group that they were being anxious for me; as Max said, I did not need safeguarding. Notice that the weight of my construction, while using language, was carried mostly by rhetorical deed – humor, expressive discourse ("yip yip yip"), and blatant irony ("don't listen to them, they are a bunch of puppies") – and by a hospitable therapeutic presence that encouraged Max's creative co-participation.

Max was the ostensible target of intervention, but I was too. At one time, I might not have encouraged Max to continue. Under the guise of clinical tactic and "correct" technique (Jacobs, 2001) I might have "analyzed" him, directing energy away from his attack and from my anxiety about being exposed. I might have called attention to Max's characteristic arrogance, likely with a slight, contemptuous flare of my nostrils. I was close enough to the "old me" to monitor myself for any disapproving taint, any whiff of counter arrogance. I recognized with relief that I had not succumbed to the talion principle, the eye-for an-eye cycle of aggression–counter aggression. Still, leading a group with less secure positive alliances towards me, I might have been in a different frame of mind: cautious with irony and metaphor, and distant from a *nuclear idea* involving assertions of "love." The supportive members lessened any vestigial need for self-protection. I could run interference for Max, countering the group's attempts to shut him down.

Doing Our Work

The maestro, Arturo Toscanini, declared: "Every time I conduct the same piece, I think how stupid I was the last time I did it" (Gottlieb, 2017, p. 20). Our work remains "in rehearsal:" perspectival, revisable, and susceptible to mutual influence and the social forces of the group and elsewhere. I was less stupid with Max than I probably would have been at one time. Still, there is no way to inoculate ourselves from stupidity, from being blindsided by assigned roles and configurations, false notes that we bring, and those thrust upon us.

However well we conduct, some notes remain dissonant, too faint, or unheard, and need of replay with our group.

> You shall no longer take things at second or third hand, nor look through the eyes of the dead, nor feed on the spectres in books… You shall listen to all sides and filter them from your self.
> (Walt Whitman. 'Song of Myself.' In *Leaves of Grass* (1855/2004))

We struggle to escape a confined mindset: speaking a voice not wholly our own, enacting scenarios directed by "spectres in books" – idealized versions of whoever we have read and guides us. With apologies to Walt Whitman, it is impossible "to filter them from yourself." The unconscious is the leader of any clinical hour, we may agree, but whose unconscious? It is *your* unconscious, in mental contact with Freud's, Klein's, Winnicott's, perhaps Bion's and Foulkes' too, resonating with the collective unconsciousness of all those who have exposed you to human wisdom and clinical work. We suffer the "anxiety of influence" (Bloom, 1997), loyalties to our predecessors, supervisors, teachers, and those earlier figures who have imprinted us with their ways of thinking and doing. If Lacan is correct in advising the analyst to guard against being "the subject supposed to know," and if Foulkes (1964) is correct that the group's desire to be led is the greatest resistance to overcome, we greatly resist too. We are attached to our leaders, love them, fight them, and fight those who challenge our attachments.

In making efforts to filter, we *need* to speak, to right (write) ourselves out of our idealized theories and theorists, trusting ourselves to deconstruct their work and create our own. Speech "communicates aspects of intrapsychic experience that can be made conscious only in action; as analysts, we may be able to locate aspects of ourselves, and hence of the patient, only after hearing ourselves speak" (Smith, 2000, p. 120). "My spoken words surprise me and teach me my thoughts" Merleau-Ponty (1964, p. 88) affirmed. Pichon-Rivière (2017, p. 106) held that the "analyst's self-analysis is organized automatically through the production of interpretations…[An] emergent [unresolved past conflict] that arises spontaneously in the analyst and must be accepted in that moment as the most important interpretation vector."

When I say "it is all about 'me'," it is to emphasize sardonically to concentrate on what we do not know about ourselves and our impact, and what we need to learn about from others. Our interventions are derived from subjective experience and *participation* in group relationships – from "speaking from the heart, with feeling…letting it come over you as you speak even if it's not fully there when you begin" (Hoffman, 2009, p. 621). Opting out of expressing subjectivity diminishes opportunities for getting it better, for feedback and discourse, for revision.

For those of you young enough, and with strong stomachs and stamina, I suggest a group of challenging adolescents, such as the one I described in *Chapter 7*. My stupidity was a rallying cry around which angry and truant adolescents could organize. In truth, I *was* stupid, until they wormed into my guts and informed my therapeutic core. This is what Winnicott meant by saying that the baby raises the family.

The old joke goes like this. The tourist asks: "How do I get to Carnegie Hall?" The New Yorker answers: "Practice, practice, practice." We practice what we preach by turning inward, attending as best we can to the discordant and concordant notes of our emotional involvement, tolerating the oscillations of paranoid-schizoid and depressive pleasure and pain. Turning outward, we try to absorb, understand, and respond to the music of other players – their leitmotifs of meaning and the effects of our mutual presence.

The ideas that we bring develop, take shape, and organize our groups. We need not be afraid of putting forth concepts and *nuclear ideas*, our focus on whatever we feel is timely and significant. Group members get drawn to a therapist who introduces and endorses complexity. A multi-level (unconscious, pre-conscious, conscious), multi-relational approach (directed to individuals, subgroups, and the whole group) stimulates, as well as investigates, intense responses. Even though there are no objective measures for what needs to be done, we assess what a person, group, or a collective is saying, what they are capable of hearing, and how best to say it. This is the essence of the art of therapy – in truth, of any activity between individuals involving learning. Strachey (1934) suggested that the curative action of psychotherapy involves reduction of the patient's harsh superego at moments of transferential intensity. To be effective and reduce the weight of guilt-inducing blame and shame, the therapist needs to be intense yet communicate a loving touch.

Individuals arrive at different points in our own development. They stay, prosper, and leave; we continue to rehearse. An accumulating history of learning and practice expresses itself in who we are and what we do. Hopefully, professional and personal development brings to the lone figure of the aging therapist less stupidity and more wisdom and savoir-faire – good luck with that!

My Relational Stance

In starting a session, I tend to wait and see where others take us. Initial and ongoing verbal and nonverbal exchanges give me a sense of each member and the group mood: "them" (individually and collectively), "me," and "us." I attempt to absorb the emotional experience of being in the group and responding to other members, all the while subject to my cohering feelings and thoughts at various levels of personal awareness. My frames of mind, both internal and group focused, shift from the moment of reunion and throughout the session; yet there is continuity too. Internal narratives unfold, associations and imagistic *reveries* connected to, or even, seemingly disconnected from anything else that is taking place. The theories and constructions by others and myself flow in and out of my mind as sources of information, mostly out. Sometimes – frequently – I feel myself irritated, troubled by something that I cannot quite identify, but which begins to occupy my mental space, even when I am otherwise engaged. Irritation, like any kind of pain, concentrates on itself, pulling its owner away from one kind of lived-in moment to another. The type of irritation I am describing is not altogether unpleasant, a demanding background noise – seductive, but also isolating. When I am fortunate, I identify a source of my irritation, and as I give it some attention, it begins to find its own being.

Symptoms "join in the conversation," Freud noted (Breuer and Freud, 1893–1895, p. 148). So I attempt to monitor mine. How loving and empathic do I feel? How benevolent, frustrated, impatient, angry, or hateful? How interested am I in myself and in the group? How am I utilizing *LHK, plus* and *minus*, to link up with others and the whole group? While there are perhaps an infinite number of subterranean themes, fantasies, and symbolic dramas (enactments), only some make *sense* (have referential salience) to which I can apply a rubric of *myth* (interpretation) with sufficient *passion* (an integration of *LHK plus/minus*). Thus, I develop a *nuclear idea* that I might offer to deepen the ongoing group process or to redirect it.

I try to do nothing without forethought yet preserve the *entitlement* to be spontaneous. I monitor the proceedings *diplomatically*, that is, attending to the nature and boundaries of interpersonal communication. Sometimes my diplomatic maneuvers – how I go about bringing people together, and structure relationships, rules, and mediums of exchange – do not jibe with the mood, beliefs, or intentions, of another, or many others. The group process may shift from the analysis of *resistance* (i.e., exploration of intrapsychic and interpersonal levels of meaning) to strategies of *rebellion*: questioning or challenging how I lead, the structures I wish to set up and maintain, and the truth goals I work for. Not infrequently, I am met with *refusal*, as an individual or the group turns away from what I offer. To maintain my *integrity*, I acknowledge differences in understanding and appreciate the legitimacies in rebellious and refusal communicative modes. Yet, in being *authentic*, I reconsider without mechanically altering what I am saying, and how I am saying it. Without preaching, I try to normalize what appears to be deviant by empathic understanding. and by universalizing diversity and showing how it may apply to all members (me included). I try to stay attuned to the outlier, the person who approaches truths that the group and I may not hear or want to hear.

When I do not have to take care of housekeeping – *bonding*, excessive dependency, protection of a member, *rebellion* or *refusal* – or even when I do – I think about what interests me in the ongoing interactions. An idea takes hold – which may relate to anything that is being expressed, or that which calls my attention in its absence. Likely, I will share my experience about this thought, linking it to occurrences that could serve as a common group reference, such as an explicit or submerged interaction pattern between members, a recurrent conflict within or outside the group, a metaphor, theme, or an aspect of one member's psychology that has general reference. I offer *nuclear ideas* with tentative conviction, to see how and if others respond and develop them further.

The best hope I have of leading a successful group is to relax, give people a sense of who I am by relating to them in a thoughtful, sometimes playful manner, and conveying that I am thinking about and trying to make sense of the group experience. I attempt to be personable and not function as a mysterious figure, invulnerable to feeling or feedback, or a know-it-all. I alter the mode of my communications and their nature to address my shifting interests, ignorance, and curiosity. Raised in the Dark Ages of classical psychoanalysis and ego psychology, I was taught: "When in doubt, shut up." Never the most obedient of students, I tended to follow the reverse, and still do. So, when I am feeling "stupid," confused or unsure, which is often, I may seek clarity from other group members, although I do not necessarily agree with or follow their guidelines.

I tend not to challenge criticism. At the same time, I remain "unwilling to act perfectly beyond a certain degree and beyond a certain length of time" (Winnicott, 1988, p. 142). The balladeer Leonard Cohen (1992) counselled: "Forget your perfect offering /There is a crack in everything /That's how the light gets in." No therapist makes a perfect offering. Ray Bradbury (1992, p. xv) captured something of our creative process: "Every morning I jump out of bed and step on a landmine. The landmine is me. After the explosion, I spend the rest of the day putting the pieces together."

However tentative, we "jump" into the clinical experience and are greeted with landmines. Some of them arise from without, but some arise from within. The work entails observing what is in front of us: the exchanges that are publicized in group discourse. At the same time, we also concentrate and self-reflect and enter into the exchanges too. We gaze inward, tolerating the "cracks" – the irruptive "emergents" (Pichon-Rivière, 2017) – that appear in our own mind while attending to the therapeutic situation.

The more work we do as leaders – the more we risk in feeling and idea – the more the group members will do independently of us, and the more likely we will be engaged in a collaborative enterprise. Something needs to happen; fresh experience needs to emerge that we witness in common and can respond to. The psychic truths that emerge should become relevant to all of us, including the leader.

Concluding Remarks: The Psychoanalytic Approach

D. N. Stern (2008, p. 184), an analytic pioneer of relational theory, confessed: "we have been dragged kicking and screaming to the realization that what really works in psychotherapy is the relationship...[theory] is the only the vehicle or springboard to create a relationship...We need to have a technique, and we cannot have a technique without a theory...but we need not delude ourselves that the technique is what achieves most of the results." "Analytical rigour: yes...But at the same time availability, openness, presence, support, receptivity" Anzieu (2021, p. 110) recently reaffirmed.

Experienced therapists, like seasoned practitioners of any discipline, are more alike than different, no matter our professed theories, institutional affiliations, and technical orientation. Our actions vary in the degree and type of verbal activity, but we tend to have a larger, not smaller, presence. We know more, and knowledge allows us to hold onto knowledge less, to express more, not less, of ourselves over time. Like all activity and inactivity by the therapist, we infringe on *and* free up each person's dependence and independence. We both contribute to and interfere with the collaborative enterprise. Isn't this true in all interpersonal relationships?

And so, there is no single psychoanalytic group approach. No clear demarcations exist even between traditional or "full" interpretations and other forms of intervention. A therapist's appreciative acknowledgment in the face of challenge may be a powerful, even decisive, interpretation, opening relational possibilities beyond the member's history and expectations. Psychoanalytic and other psychodynamic group theories offer models and metaphors for understanding others. Exploratory, tentative, even at times contradictory, our formulations enrich the relational opportunities that we offer and in which we partake. We want to be confident enough to trust our models and intuitions yet be open to reconstructing our beliefs. "Do I contradict myself?/Very well then I contradict myself/(I am large, I contain multitudes)" (Walt Whitman, 2004). We cannot rely on a psychoanalytic *Siri, Google Map*, or *Waze* to reach therapeutic goals. Wrong turns and fruitless changes of direction are expected. Some roads are rutted, others are closed for reconstruction. Enjoy the journey; someone, several, or all will join in discovering pathways for mutual growth.

References

Agazarian, Y. (1997). *Systems-Centered Therapy for Groups*. New York: Guilford.
Aguayo, J. (2009). On understanding projective identification in the treatment of psychotic states of mind: the publishing cohort of H. Rosenfeld, H. Segal and W. Bion (1946–1957). *Int. J. Psychoanal.*, 90(1): 69–90.
Agger, E. (1988). Psychoanalytic perspectives on sibling relationships. *Psychoanal., Ing.*, 8: 3–30.
Althusser, L. (1971). *Lenin and Philosophy and Other Essays*. New York: Monthly Review Press.
Anzieu, D. (1984). *The Group and the Unconscious*. London: Routledge.
Anzieu. D. (2021). Psychoanalysis still. *Int. J. Psychoanal.*, 102(1): 109–116.
Arensberg, F. (1990). Self-psychology groups. In I. Kutash and W. Wolf (Eds.), *The Group Therapist's Handbook: Contemporary Theory and Technique*. New York: Columbia University Press, pp. 135–149.
Aron, L. (1996). *A Meeting of Minds: Mutuality in Psychoanalysis*. Hillsdale, NJ: The Analytic Press.
Atlas, G. and Aron. L. (2018). *Dramatic Dialogue*. London: Routledge.
Bach, S. (2006). *Getting From Here to There: Analytic Love, Analytic Process*. Mahwah, NJ: The Analytic Press.
Balint, M. (1968). *The Basic Fault*. London: Tavistock.
Baranger, M. and Baranger, W. (2008). The analytic situation as a dynamic field. *Int. J. Psychoanal.*, 89(4): 795–826.
Baranger, M, Baranger, W., and Mom, J. (1983). Process and non-process in analytic work. *Int J Psychoanal.*, 64(1): 1–15.
Barrows, S. B. (1986, September 10). 'Mayflower Madam' Tells All. (M. Christy, Interviewer), *Boston Globe*.
Barwick, N. and Weegmann, M. (2018). *Group Therapy: A Group-Analytic Approach*. London: Routledge.

Beebe, B. and Lachmann, F. (2020). Infant research and adult treatment revised: Cocreating self-and interactive regulation. *Psychoanal. Psych.*, 37(4): 313–323.

Benhaim, D. (2008). Is there a sibling complex? *Can. J. Psychoanal.*, 16: 246–253.

Bennis, W. (2007). The challenges of leadership in the modern world: Introduction to the special issue. *Amer. Psych.*, 62(1): 2–5.

Bennis, W. G. and Shepard, H. A. (1956). A theory of group development. *Human Relations*, 9(4): 415–437.

Benjamin, J. (1988). *The Bonds of Love: Psychoanalysis Feminism, and the Problem of Domination*. New York: Pantheon.

Bergstein, A. (2019). *Bion and Meltzer's Expeditions Into Unmapped Mental Life: Beyond the Spectrum in Psychoanalysis*. New York: Routledge.

Bermudez, G. (2019). Community psychoanalysis: A contribution to an emerging paradigm. *Psychoanal. Inq.*, 39(5): 297–304.

Billow, R. M. (1997). Entitlement and counterentitlement in group psychotherapy. *Int. J. Group Psychother.*, 47(4): 459–474.

Billow, R. M. (1999a). LHK: The basis of emotion in Bion's theory. *Contemp. Psychoanal.*, 35(4): 629–646.

Billow, R. M. (1999b). An intersubjective approach to entitlement. *Psychoanal. Q.*, 68(3): 441–461.

Billow, R. M. (1999c). Power and entitlement: Or, mine versus yours. *Contemp. Psychoanal.*, 35: 473–489.

Billow, R. M. (2000a). From countertransference to "passion." *Psychoanal. Q.*, 69(1): 93–119.

Billow, R. M. (2000b). Relational levels of the container-contained in group. *Group*, 24: 243–259.

Billow, R.M. (2003). *Relational Group Psychotherapy: From Basic Assumptions to Passion*. London and Philadelphia: Jessica Kingsley Publishers.

Billow, R. M. (2004a). Truth and falsity in group. *Int. J. Group Psychother.*, 54(3): 321–345.

Billow, R. M. (2004b). A falsifying adolescent. *Psychoanal. Q.*, 73(4): 1041–1078.

Billow, R. M. (2009). Modes of leadership: Diplomacy, integrity, sincerity, and authenticity. In R. Klein, C. Rice, and V. Schermer (Eds.), *Leadership in a Changing World*. Plymouth, England: Lexington Books, pp. 29–47.

Billow, R. M. (2010a). Modes of therapeutic engagement: Part I: Diplomacy and integrity. *Int. J. Group Psychother.*, 60(1): 1–28.

Billow, R. M. (2010b). Modes of therapeutic engagement: Part II: Sincerity and authenticity. *Int. J. Group Psychother.*, 60(1): 28–58.

Billow, R. M. (2010c). *Resistance, Rebellion, and Refusal in Groups: The 3 R's.* London: Karnac.

Billow, R. M. (2010d). Anarchy. *Group Analysis*, 43(1): 65–80.

Billow, R. M. (2012a). It's all about me: Introduction to relational group psychotherapy. In J. L. Kleinberg (Ed.), *The Wiley-Blackwell handbook of group psychotherapy* (pp. 169–185). Chichester, England: John Wiley & Sons.

Billow, R. M. (2012b). It's all about "me" (behold the leader). *Int. J. Group Psychother.*, 62(4): 530–556.

Billow, R. M. (2012c). Facebook as "social fact." *Group*, 36(3): 213–222.

Billow, R. M. (2013a). The bully inside us: The gang in the mind. *Psychoanal. Inq.*, 33(2): 120–143.

Billow, R. M. (2013b). Appreciating "le non/nom." *Group Analysis*, 46(1): 33–47.

Billow, R. (2013c). Relational variations of the "container-contained." *Contemp. Psychoanal.*, 39(1): 27–50.

Billow, R. M. (2015). *Developing Nuclear Ideas: Relational Group Psychotherapy.* London: Routledge.

Billow, R. M. (2019a). Attention-getting mechanisms (AGMs): A personal journey. *Int. J. Group Psychother.*, 69(4): 408–433.

Billow, R. M. (2019b). Witnessing: The axis of the group. *Int. J. Group Psychother.*, 69(1): 54–76.

Billow, R. M. (2021a). *Richard M. Billow's Selected Papers On Psychoanalysis and Group Process: Changing Our Minds*, T. Slonim, (Ed.). London: Routledge.

Billow, R. M. (2021b). Opening Laplanche's window: Transference-countertransference in psychoanalytic group psychotherapy. *Psychoanal. Q.*, 90(2): 267–298.

Billow, R. M. (2022). Group encounters at the boundaries of developmental epochs. In Ashuach, S. and Berman, A. (Eds.), *Sibling Relations and the Horizontal Axis in Theory and Practice.* London: Routledge, pp. 11–23.

Billow, R. M. (2024a). Kaës' internal groups and actual groups: A relational perspective. *Psychoanal. Q.*, 93(3): 473–496.

Billow, R, M. (2024b). Psychodynamic group psychotherapy. In *Psychodynamic Psychotherapy: A Global Perspective.* Y. Shapiro, Ed. Hauppauge, NY: Nova, pp. 125–162.

Bion, W. R. (1961). *Experiences in Groups.* London: Tavistock.

Bion, W. R. (1962). *Learning From Experience.* London: Heinemann. Reprinted in: *Seven Servants: Four works by Wilfred R. Bion.* New York: Aronson, 1977.

Bion, W. R. (1963). *Elements of Psycho-Analysis*. London: Heinemann. Reprinted in: *Seven Servants: Four works by Wilfred R. Bion*. New York: Aronson, 1977.

Bion, W. R. (1965). *Transformations*. London: Tavistock. Reprinted in: *Seven Servants: Four Works by Wilfred R. Bion*. New York: Aronson, 1977.

Bion, W. R. (1966). Book review: Medical orthodoxy and the future of psychoanalysis, by K. R. Eissler. *Int. J. Psychoanal.*, 47: 575–579.

Bion, W. R. (1970). *Attention and Interpretation*. London: Tavistock. Reprinted in: *Seven Servants: Four Works by Wilfred R. Bion*. New York: Aronson, 1977.

Bion, W. R. (1975). *Bion's Brazilian Lectures, 2: Rio/São Paulo, 1974*. Rio de Janeiro, Brazil: Imago Editora.

Bion, W. R. (1977). *Two Papers: The Grid and Caesura*. Rio de Janeiro: Imago Editora Ltd.

Bion, W. R. (1987). *Clinical Seminars and Other Works*. F. Bion (Ed.). London: Routledge.

Bion, W. R. (1994). *Making* the best of a bad job. In F. Bion (Ed.), *Clinical Seminars and Other Works*. London: Karnac, pp. 321–332.

Bion, W. R. (1997). *Taming Wild Thoughts*, F. Bion (Ed.). London: Karnac.

Birksted-Breen, D. (2016). *The Work of Psychoanalysis: Sexuality, Time and the Psychoanalytic Mind*. London: Routledge.

Blechner, M. J. (1987). Panel II Entitlement and narcissism: Paradise sought. *Contemp. Psychoanal*, 23: 244–254.

Bloom, H. (1997). *The Anxiety of Influence* (2nd ed.). New York: Oxford University Press.

Blos, P. (1963). The concept of acting out in relation to the adolescent process. *J. Amer. Acad. Child Psychiat.*, 2(1): 118–136.

Blos, P. (1979). Adolescent concretization. In *The Adolescent Passage*. New York: Int. U. Press.

Bollas, C. (1987). *The Shadow of the Object: Psychoanalysis of the Unthought Known*. London: Free Association Books.

Boesky, D. (1990). The psychoanalytic process and its components. *Psychoanal. Q.*, 59(4): 550–584.

Bonebright, D. (2010). 40 Years of storming: a historical review of Tuckman's model of small group development. *Human Resource Development International*, 13(1): 111–120.

Bowlby, J. (1988). *A Secure Base: Parent-Child Attachment and Healthy Human Development*. New York: Basic Books.

Bradbury, R. (1992). *Zen in the Art of Writing*. New York: Bantum Books.

Breuer, J. and Freud, S. (1893–1895). *Studies on Hysteria. S. E.*: 1–335.

Bromberg, P. (2009). Multiple self states, the relational mind, and dissociation: A psychoanalytic perspective. In P. F. Dell, and J. A. O'Neill (Eds.), *Dissociation and Dissociative Disorders: DSM and Beyond* (pp. 637–652). New York, NY: Routledge.

Brown, L. (2017). Book review: *The Pioneers of Psychoanalysis in South America: An Essential Guide*, edited by Nydia Lisman-Pieczanski and Alberto Pieczanski. *Int. J. Psychoanal.*, 98(1): 266–273.

Brown, N. (2003). Conceptualizing process. *Int. J. Group Psychother.*, 53(2): 225–244.

Bucci, W. (2021). *Emotional Communication and Therapeutic Change: Understanding Psychotherapy through Multiple Code Theory.* New York: Routledge.

Butler, J. (1993). *Bodies That Matter.* New York: Routledge.

Campos Avilar, J. (1992). Burrow, Foulkes and Freud: An historical perspective. *Lifwynn Correspondence*, 2: 2–9.

Caper, R. (1997). A mind of one's own. *Int. J. Psycho-Anal.*, 78(2): 265–278.

Caputo, A. and Tomai, M. (2020). A systematic review of psychodynamic theories in community psychology: Discovering the unconscious in community work. *J. Community Psychol.*, 48(6): 2069–2085.

Chiesa, L (2007). *Subjectivity and Otherness: A Philosophical Reading of Lacan.* Cambridge, MA: MIT Press.

Cohen, B. and Schermer, V. (2002). On scapegoating in therapy groups. A social constructivist and intersubjective outlook. *Int. J. Group Psychother.*, 52(1): 89–109.

Cohen, L. (1992). "Anthem." *The Future.* New York: Columbia Records Albums.

Colonna, A. and Newman, L. (2017). The psychoanalytic literature on siblings. *Psychoanal. Study Child*, 38(1): 285–309.

Cruz, A., Sales C., Alves, P., and Moita G. (2018). The core techniques of Morenian psychodrama: A systematic review of literature. *Front. Psychol.*, 9: 1263. doi: 10.3389/fpsyg.2018.01263.

Davies, J. (1999). Dissociation, therapeutic enactment and transference-countertransference process. *Gender and Psychoanalysis*, 2: 241–259.

De Mare, P. T. (1997). The history of large group phenomena in relation to group analytic psychotherapy: The story of the median group. *Group*, 13: 173–197.

Derrida, J. (2005). *Writing and Difference.* London: Routledge.

Dickinson, E. (1960). 'Tell all the truth but tell it slant." In T. H. Johnson (Ed.), *The Complete Poems of Emily Dickinson.* Boston: Little, Brown.

Durkin, H. (1964). *The Group in Depth.* New York: Int. U. Press.

Elias, N. (1939/2000). *The Civilizing Process: Sociogenetic and Psychogenetic Investigations, Revised Edition*. E. Dunning, J. Goudsblom, and S. Mennell (Eds.), E. Jephcott (Trans.). Oxford, Eng.: Blackwell.

Einstein, A. (1922). *The Meaning of Relativity*. Princeton, NJ: Princeton University Press, 2014.

Erikson, E. (1985). Pseudospeciation in the nuclear age. *Political Psychology*, 6(2): 213–217.

Ettin, M. (1999). *Foundations and Applications of Group Psychotherapy. A Sphere of Influence*. London: Jessica Kingsley.

Ezriel, H. (1950). A psycho-analytic approach to the treatment of patients in groups. *J. of Mental Science*, 96: 774–779.

Fonagy, P. and Target, M. (1998). Mentalization and the changing aims of child psychoanalysis. *Psychoanal, Dial.*, 8: 87–114.

Fonseca, M. (2016). *Gramsci's Critique of Civil Society. Towards a New Concept of Hegemony*. New York: Routledge.

Foulkes, S. H. (1964). *Therapeutic Group Analysis*. London: George Allen & Unwin.

Foulkes, S. H. and Anthony, E. J. (1965). *Group Psychotherapy: The Psychoanalytic Approach (2nd ed)*. London: Karnac, 1984.

Foulkes, S. H. (1975). *Group Analytic Psychotherapy*. London: Karnac, 1986.

Freud, A. (1981). The concept of developmental lines. Their diagnostic significance. *Psychoanal. Study Child*, 36(1): 129–136.

Freud, S. (1894). The neuro-psychoses of defence. *S. E.* 3: 45–68.

Freud, S. (1895). A project for a scientific psychology. *S. E.* 1: 283–397.

Freud, S. (1896a). Letter 52 from the extracts from the Fliess Papers. *S. E.* 1: 233–239.

Freud, S. (1896b). Letter 70 from the extracts from the Fliess Papers. *S. E.* 1: 261–263.

Freud, S. (1905). Three essays on the theory of sexuality. *S. E.* 7: 123–244.

Freud, S. (1911). Formulations regarding the two principles in mental functioning. *S. E.* 12: 213–226.

Freud, S. (1912). Recommendations to physicians practising psycho-analysis. *S. E.* 12: 109–120.

Freud, S. (1913). *Totem and Taboo. S. E.* 13: 1–161.

Freud, S. (1914). On narcissism. *S. E.* 14: 67–102.

Freud, S. (1915). The unconscious. *S. E.* 14: 159–215.

Freud, S. (1916). Some character-types met with in psycho-analytic work. *S. E.* 14: 309–333.

Freud, S. (1921). *Group Psychology and the Analysis of the Ego. S. E.* 18: 70–92.

Freud, S. (1923). The ego and the id. *S. E.* 19: 3–70

Freud, S. (1925). A short autobiographical study. *S. E.* 20: 3–70.

Freud, S. (1926). Inhibitions, symptoms and anxiety. *S. E.* 20: 75–174.
Freud, S. (1930). *Civilization and its discontents. S. E.* 21: 57–145.
Freud, S. (1933). New introductory lectures on psycho-analysis. *S. E.* 12.
Freud, S. (1937). Constructions in analysis. *S. E.*, 32: 255–270.
Freud, S. (1938). An outline of psycho-analysis. *S. E.* 23: 144–207.
Freud, S. and Jung, C. (1974). *The Freud/Jung Letters*, R. Manheim and R. Hull (Trans.). Princeton, NJ: Princeton University Press.
Friedman, R. (2019). *Dreamtelling, Relations, and Large Groups: New Developments in Group Psychoanalytic Group.* New York: Routledge.
Garland, C. (Ed.) (2010). *The Groups Book.* London: Karnac.
Gayle, R. (2009). Co-creating meaningful structures within long-term psychotherapy group culture. *Int. J. Group Psych.*, 59(3): 311–343.
Gerson, S. (1996). Neutrality, resistance, self-disclosure. *Psychoanal. Dial.*, 6(5): 623–643.
Gerson, S. (2004). The relational unconscious: A core element of intersubjectivity, thirdness, and clinical process. *Psychoanal. Q.*, 73(1): 63–98.
Gill, M. (1994). *Psychoanalysis in Transition.* Hillsdale, NJ: Analytic Press.
Giraldo, M. (2012). *The Dialogues in and of the Group: Lacanian Perspectives on the Psychoanalytic Group.* New York: Routledge.
Goffman, E. (1959). *The Presentation of Self in Everyday Life.* New York: Doubleday Anchor Books.
González, F. J. (2020). First world problems and gated communities of the mind: An ethics of place in psychoanalysis. *Psychoanal. Q.*, 89(4): 741–770.
Gottlieb, R. (2017). 'Allegro Con Brio'. Book review of Harvey Sachs, Toscanini: Musician of Conscience. *New York Times Book Review.*
Greenberg, J. (1995). Self-disclosure: is it psychoanalytic? *Contemp. Psychoanal.*, 31(2): 193–205.
Greenberg, J. (1996). Psychoanalytic words and psychoanalytic acts: A brief history. *Contemp. Psychoanal.*, 32(2): 195–213.
Greenberg, J. (2001). The analyst's participation. *J. Amer. Psychoanal. Assoc.*, 49(2): 359–381.
Greenberg, J. (2018). Klein's technique. *Int. J. Psychoanal.*, 99(4): 979–989.
Greenberg, J. and Mitchell, S. (1983) *Object Relations in Psychoanalytic Theory.* Cambridge, MA: Harvard University Press.
Greenson, R. R. (1967). *The Technique and Practice of Psychoanalysis.* New York: International Universities Press.
Grice, H. P. (1989). *Studies in the Way of Words.* Cambridge, MA: Harvard University Press.
Grossmark, R. (2007). The edge of chaos: Enactment, disruption, and emergence in group therapy. *Psychoanalytic Dialogues*, 17(4): 479–499.

Grotjahn, M. (1977). *Art and Technique of Analytic Group Therapy*. New York: Jason Aronson.

Grotstein, J. S. (1995). American view of the British psychoanalytic experience: Psychoanalysis in counterpoint. *Fort Da*, 1: 4–10.

Guess, R. (1981) *The Idea of a Critical Theory. Habermas & the Frankfurt School*. New York: Cambridge University Press.

Guntrip, H. (1975). My experience of analysis with Fairbairn and Winnicott (how complete a result does psychoanalytic therapy achieve?). *Int. Rev. Psychoanal.*, 2: 145–156.

Harwood, I. and Pines, M. (1998). *Self-Experiences in Group: Intersubjective and Self Psychological Pathways to Human Understanding*. London: Jessica Kingsley Publishers.

Hoffman, I. Z. (1994). Dialectical thinking and therapeutic action in the psychoanalytic process. *Psychoanal. Q.*, 63(2): 187–218.

Hoffman. I. Z. (2009). Therapeutic passion in the countertransference. *Psychoanal, Dial.*, 19(5): 617–637.

Hopper, E. (1997). Traumatic experience in the unconscious life of groups: a fourth basic assumption. *Group Anal.*, 30(4): 439–470.

Hopper, E. (2003). *The Social Unconscious: Selected Papers*. London and Philadelphia: Jessica Kingsley Publishers.

Horwitz, L. (1977). A group-centered approach to group psychotherapy. *Int. J. Group Psycho.*, 27(4): 423–439.

Isakower, O. (1992). The analyzing instrument: Further thoughts. *J. Cl. Psychoanal.*, 1: 200–203.

Jacobs, T. (1986). On countertransference enactments. *J. Am. Psychoanal. Assoc.*, 34(2): 289–307.

Jacobs, T. (1992). Isakower's ideas of the analytic instrument and contemporary views of analytic listening. *J. Cl. Psychoanal.*, 1: 237–241.

Jacobs, T. (2001). On misreading and misleading patients: Some reflections on communication, miscommunications and countertransference enactments. *Int J. Psychoanal.*, 82(4): 653–669.

Jones, E. (1955). *The Life and Work of Sigmund Freud: Volume 1 The Formative Years and the Great Discoveries 1856–1900*. London: Hogarth.

Kaës, R. (1993). *La Groupe et le Sujet du Groupe. Elements pour une Theorie Psychoanalytiques des Groups*. Paris: Dunod.

Kaës, R. (2007). *Linking, Alliances and Shared Space. Groups and the Psychoanalyst*. London: International Psychoanalysis Library.

Kaës, R. (2016a). The influence of Bion on my research. In H. B. Levine and G. Civitarese (Eds.), *The W.R. Bion Tradition*. London: Routledge, pp. 431–446.

Kaës, R. (2016b). Link and transference within three interfering psychic spaces. *Couples & Fam. Psychoanal.*, 6: 181–193.

Kaës, R. (2017). Meeting Pichon-Rivière. In R. Losso, L. de Setton, and D. Scharff (Eds.), *The Linked Self in Psychoanalysis: The Pioneering Work of Enrique Pichon-Rivière*. London: Routledge.

Kahn, M. (2014). The intransience of the sibling bond: a relational and family systems view. In B.Maciejewska, K.Katarzyna, K. Skrzypek, and Z.Stadnicka-Dmitriew (Eds.), *Siblings: Envy and Rivalry, Coexistence and Concern*. London: Karnac, pp. 41–56.

Karen, R. (2024). *Becoming Attached*. New York: Oxford.

Kelly, K. (1997). Classics revisited: Heinrich Racker's Transference and Countertransference. *J. Amer. Psychoanal. Assn.*, 45(4): 1253–1259.

Kernberg, O. (2000). A concerned critique of psychoanalytic education. *Int. J. Psychoanal.*, 81(1): 97–120.

Kieffer, C. (2014). *Mutuality, Recognition, and the Self: Psychoanalytic Reflections*. London: Karnac.

Kirshner, L. (2006). The work of Rene Kaës: Intersubjective transmission in families, groups, and culture. *J. Amer. Psychoanal. Assoc.*, 54(3): 1005–1013.

Kirshner, L. (2015). The translational metaphor in psychoanalysis. *Int. J. Psychoanal.*, 96(1): 65–81.

Kirshner, L. (2017). *Intersubjectivity in Psychoanalysis*. New York: Routledge.

Klein, M. (1952). Some theoretical conclusions regarding the emotional life of the infant. In Klein, M. (1975), *Envy and Gratitude and Other Works 1946–1963. Vol. III*. New York: Delacorte Press, pp. 61–93.

Klein, M. (1957). Envy and gratitude. In Klein, M. (1975). *Envy and Gratitude and Other Works 1946–1963. Vol. III*. New York: Delacorte Press, pp. 176–235.

Koenig, K. and Lindner, W.-V. (1994). *Psychoanalytic Group Therapy*. Northvale, NJ: Aronson.

Kohon, G. and Perelberg, R. (Eds.) (2018). *The Greening of Psychoanalysis: Andre Green's New Paradigm in Contemporary Theory and Practice 1st Edition*. New York: Routledge.

Kohut, H. (1991). On empathy. In P. Ornstein (Ed.), *The Search for the Self: Selected Writings of Heinz Kohut, 1978–1981*. Madison, CT: International Universities Press, 525–536.

Kreeger, L. (Ed.) (1975). *The Large Group, Dynamics and Therapy*. London: Karnac.

Lacan, J. (1938). Family. 1. The complex, a concrete factor in psychology. *Encyclopedia Francaise*, 8: 840–848.

Lacan, J. (1947). British psychiatry and the war. *Psychoanalytic Notebooks of the London Circle*, 4: 9–34.

Lacan, J. (1953–77). *The Seminar of Jacques Lacan—Book II: The Ego in Freud's Theory and in the Technique of Psychoanalysis, 1954–1955*, J. A.

Miller, (Ed.), John Forrester (Trans.). Cambridge: Cambridge University Press, 1988.

Lacan, J. (1967/2002). *The Seminar of Jacques Lacan. Book XIV: The Logic of Phantasy.* London: Karnac.

Lacan, J. (1977). *The Four Fundamental Concepts of Psycho-Analysis.* London: Tavistock.

Lacan, J. (1978). *The Four Fundamental Concepts of Psycho-Analysis*, Alain Miller (Ed.); Alan Sheridan (Trans.). New York: W. W. Norton.

Laplanche, J. (1992). The drive and its object source: its fate in the transference. In *Jean Laplanche: Seduction, Translation and the Drives.* J. Fletcher and M. Stanton (Eds.), M. Stanton (Trans.). London: Psychoanalytic Forum, Institute of Contemporary Arts, pp. 179–195.

Laplanche, J. (1999). *Essays on Otherness*, J. Fletcher (Ed.). London: Routledge.

Laplanche, J. and Pontalis, J. B. (1973). *The Language of Psychoanalysis.* New York: Norton.

Lawrence, W. G. (2005). *An Introduction to Social Dreaming.* London: Karnac.

Layton, L. (2020). *Toward a Social Psychoanalysis: Culture, Character, and Normative Unconscious*, Marianna Leavy-Sperounis (Ed.). New York: Routledge.

Leiderman, M. and Buchele, B. (Eds.) (2025). *Advances in Group Therapy Trauma Treatment.* New York: Routledge.

Levi, P. (1996). *Survival In Auschwitz.* S. Woolf (Trans.). New York: Touchstone.

Levin, C. (2008) The sibling complex. Thoughts on French-English "translation." *Canad. J. Psychoanal.*, 16: 262–274.

Levine, R. (2011). Progressing while regressing in relationships. *Int. J. Group Psychother.*, 61(4): 621–642.

Levine, H. (2022). Staring into the abyss: Encountering and transforming the unrepresented and inaccessible. *J. Am. Psychoanal. Assoc.*, 70(1): 187–204.

Levine, H. B. (2023). A Metapsychology of the unrepresented. *Psychoanal. Q.*, 92(1): 11–25.

Levine, H. B., Reed, G. S., and Scarfone, D. (Eds.) (2018). *Unrepresented States and the Construction of Meaning: Clinical and Theoretical Contributions.* New York: Routledge.

Long, S. and Manley, J. (Eds.) (2019). *Social Dreaming: Philosophy, Research, Theory and Practice.* London: Routledge.

Losso, R., de Setton, L., and Scharff, D. (Eds.) (2017). *The Linked Self in Psychoanalysis: The Pioneering Work of Enrique Pichon-Rivière.* London: Routledge.

Lykes, M. and Moane, G. (2009). Whither feminist liberation psychology? Critical exploration of feminist and liberation psychologies for a globalizing world. *Feminism & Psychol.*, 19(3): 283–298.

Lyons-Ruth, K. (1999). The two-person unconscious: Intersubjective dialogue, enactive relational representation, and the emergence of new forms of relational organization. *Psychoanal. Inq.*, 19(4): 576–617.

Macnair-Semands, R., Ogrodniczuck, J., and Joyce, A. (2010). Structure and initial validation of a short form of the therapeutic factors inventory. *Int. J. Group. Psychother.*, 60(2): 245–281.

Martin-Baro, I. (1994). *Writings for Liberation Psychology*, Adrianne Aron and Shawn Corne (Eds.). Cambridge, MA: Harvard University Press.

Matte-Blanco, I. (1988). *Thinking, Feeling, and Being: Clinical Reflections on the Fundamental Antinomy of Human Beings and World*. London: Taylor & Francis/Routledge.

McLaughlin, J. T. (1991). Clinical and theoretical aspects of enactment. *J. Am. Psychoanal. Assoc.*, 39(3): 595–614.

Meissner, W. (1976). Schreber and the paranoid process. *Annual of Psychoanal.*, 4: 3–40.

Merleau-Ponty, M. (1964). *Signs*. Evanston, IL: Northwestern Universities Press.

Michels, R. (1988). The psychology of rights. In V. D. Volkan and T. C. Rogers (Eds.), *Attitudes of Entitlement*. Charlottesville, VA: University Press of Virginia, pp. 53–62.

Mitchell, J. (2003). *Siblings*. Oxford, England: Polity Press.

Mitchell, J. (2013). Siblings: Thinking theory. *Psychoanal. St. Child*, 67(1): 14–34.

Mitchell, S. and Black, M. (1996). *Freud And Beyond: A History of Modern Psychoanalytic Thought*. New York: Basic Books.

Modell, A. H. (1976). *The holding environment and the therapeutic action of psychoanalysis. In: Classics in Psychoanalytic Technique*, R. Langs (Ed.). New York: Aronson, 1981, pp. 489–498.

Moreno, J. L. (1952). Psychodramatic production techniques. *Group Psychotherapy, Psychodrama & Sociometry*, 4: 273–303.

Nathanson, D. (2008). Prologue. In S. S. Tomkins (Ed.), *Affect, Imagery, Consciousness: The Complete Edition*. New York: Springer, pp. xi–xxvi.

Newirth, J. (2023). *The Unconscious: A Contemporary Introduction*. London: Routledge.

Nitsun, M. (1996). *The Anti-Group: Destructive Forces in the Group and their Creative Potential*. London: Routledge.

Nitsun, M. (2015). *Beyond the Anti-Group*. London: Routledge.

Ogden, T. H. (1989). *The Primitive Edge of Experience*. Northvale, NJ: Aronson.

Ogden, T. (2011). Reading Susan Isaacs: Toward a radically revised theory of thinking. *Int. J. Psychoanal.*, 92: 925–942.

Ormont, L. (1992). *The Group Therapy Experience*. New York: St. Martins.

Paredes, D. (2015). Psychodrama. In E. W. Neukrug (Ed.), *The Sage Encyclopedia of Theory in Counseling and Psychotherapy*. Los Angeles: Sage, pp. 812–816.

Pertegato, E. and Pertegato, G. (Eds.) (2013). *From Psychoanalysis to the Group. The Pioneering Work of Trigant Burrow*. London: Karnac.

Pichon-Rivière, E. (2017). Part I: Pichon- Rivière's Writings. In R. Losso, L. de Setton, and D. Scharff (Eds.) *The Linked Self in Psychoanalysis: The Pioneering Work of Enrique Pichon-Rivière*. London: Routledge, pp. 3–137.

Pines, M. (2010). Cohesion and coherency in Group Analysis. *Group Analysis*, 43(4): 496–504.

Pines, M. and Marrone, M. (1990). Group analysis. In I. Kutash and W. Wolf (Eds.), *The Group Therapist's Handbook: Contemporary Theory and Technique*. New York: Columbia U. Press, pp. 61–77.

Powell, A. (1994). Towards a unifying concept of the group matrix. In, *The Psyche and the Social World: Developments in Group-Analytic Theory*, D. Brown and L. Zinkin (Eds.). London: Routledge, pp. 11–26.

Racker, H. (1968). *Transference and Countertransference*. Madison, CT: International Universities Press.

Raphael-Leff, J. (1990). If Oedipus was an Egyptian. *Int. Rev. of Psychoanal.*, 17: 309–317.

Reis, B. (2009). Performative and enactive features of psychoanalytic witnessing: The transference as the scene of address. *Int. J. Psychoanal.*, 90: 1359–1372.

Renik. O. (1993). Analytic interaction: Conceptualizing technique in light of the analyst's irreducible subjectivity. *Psychoanal. Q.*, 62(4): 553–571.

Rescher, N. (1987). *Forbidden Knowledge and other Essays on the Philosophy of Cognition*. Dordrecht, Germany: Reidel.

Romero-Garcia, M. (2021). The Social Within: Pichon-Rivière, Vinculo, & the Spiral Process. Dissertation, Graduate School of Applied and Professional Psychology, Rutgers University. https://rucore.libraries.rutgers.edu/rutgers-lib/66462/PDF/1/play/.

Rowan, A. and Harper, E. (1999). Group subversion as subjective necessity–Towards a Lacanian orientation to psychoanalysis in group settings. In C. Oakley (Ed.), *What is a Group? A New Look at Theory in Practice*. London: Rebus, pp. 168–203.

Rudnytsky, P., Bokay, A., and Giampieri-Deutsch, P. (Eds.) (1996). *Ferenczi's Turn in Psychoanalysis*. New York: New York Universities Press.

Rutan, J. S., Stone, W., and Shay, J. (2014). *Psychodynamic Group Therapy (5th ed)*. New York: Guilford Press.

Sacks, J. (1990) Psychodrama. In I. Kutash and W. Wolf (Eds.), *The Group Therapist's Handbook: Contemporary Theory and Technique.* New York: Columbia U. Press, pp. 211–230.

Sandler, J. (1976). Countertransference and role responsiveness. *Int. Rev. Psychoanal.*, 3: 43–47.

Scharff, D., Losso, R., and Setton, L. (2017). Pichon Rivière's psychoanalytic contributions: Some comparisons with object relations and modern developments in psychoanalysis. *Int. J. Psychoanal.*, 98(1): 129–143.

Scheidlinger, S. (1964). Identification, the sense of belonging and of identity in small groups. *Int. J. Group Psychother.*, 14(3): 291–306.

Schlapobersky, J. (2016). *From the Couch to the Circle: Group-Analytic Psychotherapy in Practice.* London: Routledge.

Schneider, S. and Weinberg, H. (Eds.) (2003). *The Large Group Re-Visited: The Herd, Primal Horde, Crowds and Masses.* London: Jessica Kingsley Publishers.

Searles, H. F. (1979). *Countertransference and Related Subjects.* New York: International Universities Press.

Seligman, S. (2003). The developmental perspective in relational psychoanalysis. *Contemp. Psychoanal.*, 39(3): 477–508.

Skynner, A. (1983). Group analysis and family therapy. In M. Pines (Ed.), *The Evolution of Group Analysis.* London: Routledge.

Slavson, S. (1957/1992). Are there "group dynamics" in therapy groups? *Classics in Group Psychotherapy*, K. Roy Mackenzie (Ed.). New York: Guilford Press, pp. 166–182.

Slavson, S. (1964). *A Textbook in Analytic Group Therapy.* New York: Int. U. Press.

Smith, H. (2000). Countertransference, conflictual listening, and the analytic object relationship. *J. Am. Psychoanal. Assoc.*, 48(1): 95–128.

Spotnitz, H. and Meadow, P. (1976). *Treatment of the Narcissistic Neuroses.* New York: The Manhattan Center for Advanced Psychoanalytic Studies.

Stern, D. B. (2019). *The Infinity of the Unsaid: Unformulated Experience, Language, and the Nonverbal.* New York: Routledge.

Stern, D. N. (2008). The clinical relevance of infancy: A progress report. *Infant Mental Health Journal*, 29(3): 177–188.

Stern, D. N., Sander, L. W., Nahum, J. P., Harrison, A. M., Lyons-Ruth, K., Morgan, A. C., and Bruschweiler-Stern, D. N. (1998). Non-interpretive mechanisms in psychoanalytic therapy: The "something more" than interpretation. *Int. J. Psychoanal.*, 79(5): 903–921.

Stolorow, R., Magid, B., Fosshage, J., and Shane, E. (2021). The emerging paradigm of relational self psychology: An historical perspective, *Psychoanal., Self and Context*, 16(1): 1–23.

Strachey, J. (1934). The nature of the therapeutic action of psychoanalysis. *Int. J. Psychoanal.*, 15: 127–159.

Sullivan, H. S. (1953). *The Interpersonal Theory of Psychiatry*. New York: Norton.

Symington, N. (1983). The analyst's act of freedom as agent of therapeutic change. *Int. Rev. Psychoanal.*, 10: 783–792.

Thoma, H. and Kachele, H. (1994). *Psychoanalytic Practice: Volume 1. Principles*. Northvale, NJ: Aronson.

Thomas, D. (1954). *A Child's Christmas in Wales*. New York: New Directions.

Tomkins, S. S. (1995). *Exploring Affect*, E. V. Demos, (Ed.). Cambridge, UK: Cambridge University Press.

Trilling, L. (1972). *Sincerity and Authenticity*. Cambridge: Harvard University Press.

Tubert-Oklander, J. (2011). Lost in translation: A contribution to intercultural understanding. *Can. J. Psychoanal.*, 19(1): 144–168.

Tubert-Oklander, J. and Hernández de Tubert, R. (2004). *Operative Groups: The Latin-American Approach to Group Analysis*. London: Jessica Kingsley.

Tuckman, B. W. (1965). Developmental sequences in small groups. *Psych. Bull.*, 63(6): 384–399.

Volkan, V. D. (1988). *The Need to Have Enemies and Allies: From Clinical Practice to International Relationships*. Northvale, NJ: Jason Aronson.

Wallerstein, R. (1990). Psychoanalysis: The common ground. *Int. J. Psychoanal.*, 71: 3–20.

Weiss, J., Simpson, H., and the Mount Zion Psychotherapy Research Group. (1986). *The Psychoanalytic Process: Theory, Clinical Observation, and Empirical Research*. New York: Guilford.

Whitaker, D. (1989). Group focal conflict theory: Description, illustration and evaluation. *Group*, 13(3-4): 225–251.

Whitaker, D. and Lieberman, M. (1964). *Psychotherapy Through the Group Process*. New York: Prentice-Hall.

Whitman, W. (2004). "Song of myself." In F. Murphy (Ed.), *The Complete Poems*. London: Penguin Classics.

Winnicott, D. W. (1949). Hate in the countertransference. *Int. J. Psychoanal.*, 30: 69–74.

Winnicott, D. W. (1965). *Maturational Processes and the Facilitating Environment*. London: Hogarth Press.

Winnicott, D. W. (1971). *Playing and Reality*. London: Tavistock.

Winnicott, D. W. (1974). Fear of breakdown. *Int. Rev. Psychoanal.*, 1(1–2): 103–107.
Winnicott, D. W. (1988). *Human Nature*. New York: Schocken.
Wolf, A. and Schwartz, E. (1962). *Psychoanalysis in Groups*. New York: Grune & Stratton.
Wren, D. and Greenwood, R. (1998). *Management Innovators: The People and Ideas That Have Shaped Modern Business*. Oxford: Oxford U. Press.
Yalom, I. (1995). *The Theory and Practice of Group Psychotherapy* (Fourth ed.). New York: Basic Books.
Yalom, I. and Leszcz, M. (2020). *The Theory and Practice of Group Psychotherapy* (Sixth ed.). New York: Basic Books.
Zeisel, E. (2012). Meeting maturational needs in *Modern Group Analysis*: A schema for personality integration and interpersonal effeciveness. In J. L. Kleinberg (Ed.), *The Wiley-Blackwell Handbook of Group psychotherapy*. Chichester, England: John Wiley & Sons, Ltd., pp. 217–249.

Index

accommodating – interpretating 101–104
actual groups 25, 59, 72–73
affects, basic 59–62
Agazarian, Y. 29–30
Agger, E. 71
aggression: in conflict and growth models 49–50; expression of 22
A.K. Rice Institute (AKRI) 29
Althusser, L. 24
American Group Psychoanalytic Association 16
American Psychoanalytic Association 12
analytic field 26
anarchy 66
Anthony, E.J. 106, 115
anti-linking communications as variation of container-contained 91–92, 94–95
anxiety, therapist's 4–6
Anzieu, D. 30, 39, 71, 124
Aron, L. 45, 50
assumptions: held by therapists 10; shared by psychodynamic group psychotherapies 12–15; *see also* basic assumptions
attachment, biological basis of 32–33
authenticity 99–100, 103
authority phase of groups 30
author's perspective 8–10

axes, vertical and horizontal 25

Bach, S. 115
Balint, M. 89
Barangers, M. and W. 9, 25, 26
Barrows, S.B. 97
basic affects 59–62
basic assumptions 26, 58, 66, 67, 78, 86, 93; group development and 56; Incohesion: Aggregation/Massification (I:AM) 19; psychotic/normal personality 28
behavioral approach, pressure for 13
Bennis, W. 30, 63, 81
biological basis of attachment 32–33
Bion, W.R. 5, 7, 9, 15, 48, 49, 54, 60, 74, 75, 77, 84, 115; artist, analyst as 52; basic assumptions 8, 26, 28, 58, 66, 67, 86; group therapy and 11–12; human emotion 59–60; metapsychological framework 84–87; protomental phenomena 51; psychoanalytic objects, concept of 105–106; qualities of psychoanalytic objects 109–110; relational variations of container-contained 87–95; Tavistock/Human Relations Groups 28–29
Birksted-Breen, D. 50
Blechner, M. J. 101

Boesky, D. 48
bonding variation of container-contained 89–91, 94, 95
boundaries of the group, external/internal 55
Bowlby, J. 32
Breuer, J. and Freud, S. 122
bridging 22–23
Bromberg, P. 58
Bucci, W. 59
Butler, J. 34

case presentations by therapists 9–10
Center for Group Studies (CGS) 23
Center for Modern Psychoanalytic Studies (CMPS) 23
challenges of group psychotherapy 3
classic psychoanalytic model 16–17
clinical examples by therapists 9–10
cognitive-developmental psychology 32–33
Cohen, B. 98
combined individual-group therapy 41–43
communication: fixed narratives 83; fixed patterns of 82–84; human, nature of 81; irruptive reactions 83–84; polarized thinking and behavior 83; traumatized members 83
condensation 106
confidentiality 44
configuration, group participants as forming 18
conformity to group norms 54
container-contained: anti-linking communications 91–92, 94–95; bonding variation of 89–91, 94, 95; relational variations of 87–95; retranscribing 74–75; symbolic communications 91, 94, 95; truth seeking 87–95
contemporary psychoanalytic model 16–17

contemporary therapy: common denominators in group approaches 34–35; convergences in 34
contracts, group 22–23
convergences in contemporary therapy 34
countertransference, transference- 47–48
Critical Theory 33

deconstructive-reconstructive group process 111–115
Derrida, J. 112
diachronic models of mental growth 55
diplomacy 95–97, 103
discourse and free association 45–46
disposition points 25
down-to-earth, being 9
drives, primary 60–62
dual axes theory 71–74
Durkin, H. 16
dynamic matrix 18; of social dreaming 19

education, psychoanalytic 12, 15
Elias, N. 17–18
emergents 25–26
emotional communication 22–23
emotional thoughts 106
emotions, basic affects and 59–62
enactments 46–47
encounter groups 27
enigmatic messages 24, 59, 109
entitlement 100–104
Erikson, E. 54
evasive responses 85
external boundaries of the group 55
extra-group communications 44

factual/psychic truth 84–87
Field Theory 27
fixed narratives 83
fixed patterns of communication 82–84

formative, reactive, mature, and termination model 56
forming, storming, norming, performing and adjourning 56
Foulkes, S.H. 3, 49–50, 67, 106, 113, 115, 119; Group Analytic model 17–19
foundation matrix 18
Frankfurt School of Critical Theory 33
free association 45–46
French psychoanalytic model 23–25
Freud, A. 58, 85
Freud, S. 7, 21–22, 46, 49, 51–52, 54, 55, 72, 101, 115; affects 60; and Breuer, J. 122; deconstruction 111–115; group psychotherapy and 3; on group therapy 11; impact of 12–13; implicit messages from carers 24; *nachtraglichkeit* (afterwardness) 24, 76; Oedipus complex 15; primary/secondary process thinking 57–58; psychoanalytic model 16–17; resistance 63, 64; resistance, group therapy and 14; sibling complex 69–71; transference 47; transference, group therapy and 14
frustration 101
functional subgroups 29

Garland, C. 15, 40
Gerson, S. 44, 46
gestalt-informed neurological perspective 17
G – group forces 53–54
Gide, A. 98
Gill, M. 14, 44
Goffman, E. 82
Goldstein, K. 17
gratification 101
Greenberg, J. 26, 31, 32, 46, 66
Greenson, R. 44
Grice, P. 113
Grossmark, R. 17, 83

groupality 24–25
Group Analytic model 17–19; modern 21–23
group contracts 22–23
group dynamic models 26–31
group dynamics 16–17
group process: basic affects 59–62; G – group forces 53–54; group vs therapist-centered 67–68; as imaginary concept with experiental properties 55; internal/actual groups 59; interplay of mental categories 57–59; metaphorical concepts of 55; phases of 55–57; stages of group development 55–57; 3Rs: resistance, rebellion and refusal 62–67
group psychotherapy, challenges of 3
group system 29
group vs therapist-centered groups 67–68
Guntrip, H. 69

hard-to-reach individuals 39–40
hate 50
healing process in group therapy 18
history of group therapy movement: classic psychoanalytic model 16–17; cognitive-developmental psychology 32–33; convergences in contemporary therapy 34; French psychoanalytic model 23–25; Group Analytic model 17–19; group dynamic models 26–31; interpersonal model 20–21; intersubjective model 19–20; models 16; Modern Group Analysis 21–23; operative groups 25–26; psychoanalytic models 16–26; psychodrama 30–31; relational turn in psychoanalytic thinking 31–34; self-psychological group approach 19–20; system-

centered therapy 29–30; Tavistock/Human Relations Groups 28–29
Hopper, E. ix, 17, 18, 19, 35
horizontal axis 25
Human Relations Groups 28–29

I:AM (Incohesion: Aggregation/Massification) 19
idealizations 20
ideas, nuclear 9
Imaginary order 24
impasses and opportunities: entitlement 100–104; fixed patterns of communication 82–84; relational variations of container-contained 87–95; strategies of therapeutic discourse 95–100; truth and falsity 81, 84–87
implication 113
implicit messages from carers 24
Incohesion: Aggregation/Massification (I:AM) 19
indirect speech acts 113
infancy: developmental stages of 30; research 32–33
infant-mother interactions 32–33
institutional psychoanalysis: group therapy and 11; schisms in, results of 13
integrity 97–98, 103
internal boundaries of the group 55
internal groups 24–25, 26, 59, 72–73
International Association for Group Psychotherapy and Group Process (IAGP) 13
interpellation 24
interpersonal model 20–21
interplay of mental categories 57–59
interpretating – accommodating 101–104
intersubjective factors of psychoanalysis 34
intersubjective model 19–20
interventions in group therapy 4

intimacy phase of groups 30
irruptive reactions 83–84

Jacobs, T. 17, 116, 118
Johnson, S. 97
Jung, C. 50

Kaës, R. 23, 24–25, 71–74
Kant, I. 51
Kernberg, O. 12
Kieffer, C. 71
Kierkegaard, S. 46
Kirshner, L. 46, 72,
Klein, M. 7, 12, 28, 33, 46, 55, 58, 60
Kohon, G. 35, 83
Kohut, H. 19–20, 46, 101
Kreeger, L. 19

Lacan, J. 23, 24, 40, 49, 51, 85, 113, 116, 119
Laplanche, J. 23, 49
Large Group experiences 19
Lawrence, G. 19
Leszcz, M. 21
Levi, P. 83
Lewin, K. 27, 53, 54
LHK: love, hate, knowledge as primary drives 60–62
linear models of mental growth 55, 56
living human systems theory 29–30
long-term groups, new members and 56–57
love, hate and knowledge (LHK) as primary drives 60–62
loving therapeutic relationship 115–118

Marrone, M. 14
Martin-Baro, I. 34
mature stage of groups 56
membership of groups 39–41
member systems 29
mental categories, interplay of 57–59
mentalization 7–8
Merleau-Ponty, M. 120

metapsychological framework, Bion's 84–87
Michels, R. 101
mirroring 20
misalliances 59
Mitchell, J. 31, 32, 70, 73–74, 75
Modell, A.H. 103
Modern Group Analysis 21–23
moral order of a group 98
Moreno, J.L. 14, 30, 31
multiple code model of thinking 59
multiple self-state model 58
myth, psychoanalytic objects and 109

nachtraglichkeit (afterwardness) 24, 76–77
narcissism, healthy, development of 19–20
narratives, fixed 83
neurological perspective 17
neutrality 44
new groups 56
new members 40; in open groups 56–57
Nietzsche, F. 100
non-psychologically-minded individuals 39–40
nonverbal containment 5
nuclear ideas 9, 106–109

Oedipus complex 15
open groups, new members and 56–57
operative groups 25–26
opinions 106
opportunities and impasses: entitlement 100–104; fixed patterns of communication 82–84; relational variations of container-contained 87–95; strategies of therapeutic discourse 95–100; truth and falsity 81, 84–87
organizational group therapy, schisms in, results of 13

Ormont, L. 22–23

passion, psychoanalytic objects and 110
Perelberg, R. 35, 83
personality, psychotic/normal 28
personal matrix 18
person systems 29
phases of group development 30, 55–57
Pichon-Rivière, E. 7, 14, 15, 120; operative groups 25–26
Pines, M. 14, 17, 18–19
polarized thinking and behavior 83
politically-oriented theorists 34
Powell, A. 55
premonitory anxiety 60
preparation for groups 40
presentation of the self 82
presentations by therapists 9–10
primary drives 60–62
primary/secondary process thinking 57–58
pseudospeciation 54
psi (Ψ) communications 85–86
psychic/factual truth 84–87
psychic matrix 18
psychic phases 56
psychoanalytic, group psychotherapy as 11–15
psychoanalytically-informed approaches, renaissance of 13–14
psychoanalytic education 12, 15
psychoanalytic function of the personality 7–8
psychoanalytic models, group therapy movement and 16–26
psychoanalytic objects, groups as: concept of 105–106; deconstructive-reconstructive group process 111–115; loving therapeutic relationship 115–118; myth 109; nuclear ideas and 106–109; passion 1110; qualities of 109–110; relational stance

121–124; sense 109; work of the therapist 119–121
psychodrama 30–31
psychopharmacological approach, pressure for 13
psychotic/normal personality 28
purpose of groups 105

Racker, H. 26, 115
Rapheal-Leff, J. 70
reactive stage of groups 56
reality testing 48–49
rebellion 62–63, 65–66
refusal 9, 62, 66–67
relational group psychotherapy 17
relational psychoanalysis 23–25
relational turn in psychoanalytic thinking 31–34
relational unconscious 46
Renik, O. 48
Rescher, N. 67
resistance 63–65; 3Rs – resistance, rebellion and refusal 9, 62–67; group therapy and 14; to joining groups 40–41; therapist's 4–6
reverie 51, 52
Rice, A.K. 29
Rogers, C. 27
Rutan, J.S. 56

Scheidlinger, S. 115
Schermer, V. 98
scientific papers by therapists 9–10
Searles, H.F. 89
self-disclosure 44–45
self-knowledge 97
self-psychological group approach 19–20
self-reflections 106
sense, psychoanalytic objects and 109
sensitivity group movement 27
Shay, J. 56
siblings: container-contained 74–75; dual axes theory 71–74; Freud's sibling complex 69–71; as part of therapeutic process 69; psychoanalysis, sibling complex and 70–71
sincerity 98–99, 103
Skynner, A. 14
Slavson, S. 16, 67
small talk 82
Smith, H. 50, 120
Social Dreaming Group 19
Social Dreaming International Network (SDIN) 19
social unconscious 18, 19
sociologically-oriented theorists 34
sociometry 31
speech acts 113
spiral learning process 25–26
Spotnitz, H. 21–22, 23
stages of group development 30, 55–57
stereotype subgroups 29
Stern, D.B. 51, 58
Stern, D.N. 47, 124
Stone, W. 56
Strachey, J. 121
strategies of therapeutic discourse: authenticity 99–100; diplomacy 95–97; integrity 97–98; sincerity 98–99
subgroup systems 29
subjectivity of therapists 48
subsymbolic systems 59
Sullivan, H.S. 21, 31, 32, 58, 74
symbolic communications as variation of container-contained 91, 94, 95
symbolic meanings in discourse 109
symbolic systems 59
synchronic models of mental growth 55–56
system-centered therapy 29–30

Tavistock/Human Relations Groups 28–29
termination stage of groups 56
testing reality 48–49

textbooks on group analysis 14
therapeutic discourse, strategies of: authenticity 99–100; diplomacy 95–97; integrity 97–98; sincerity 98–99
therapists: aggression 50; anxiety of 4–6; as container/contained 75; group vs therapist-centered groups 67–68; neutrality 44; position of in group therapy 4; relational turn in psychoanalytic thinking 32; resistance to group therapy 4–6; self-disclosure 44–45; self-presentation and 86–87; subjectivity of 48
Thomas, D. 70
3Rs: resistance, rebellion and refusal 9, 62–67
three-way relationships in groups 15
Tomkins, S.S. 61
training, psychoanalytic 12
training groups 27
transference, group therapy and 14
transference-countertransference 47–48
transmuting internalizations 20
traumatized members 83
triangular relationships in groups 15
tribalism 54

Trilling, L. 99
trust/distrust 44
truth: container-contained 87–95; evasion 81; and falsity 84–87; strategies of therapeutic discourse 95–100
Tubert-Oklander, J. 26, 72
Tuckman, B.W. 56
twinship 20

unconscious alliances 59
unrepresented/unrepresentable states of mental experience 50–52

valency 54
vertical axis 25

Whitaker, D. 48, 109
Whitman, W. 119
Wilde, O. 98
Winnicott, D.W. 20, 50, 72, 89, 101, 114, 120
witnessing 83
workgroup mentality 28, 56, 58, 66–67, 93
work phase of groups 30

Yalom, I. 20–21, 67, 115

Zeisel, E. 23, 50

For Product Safety Concerns and Information please contact our EU representative GPSR@taylorandfrancis.com
Taylor & Francis Verlag GmbH, Kaufingerstraße 24, 80331 München, Germany

www.ingramcontent.com/pod-product-compliance
Ingram Content Group UK Ltd.
Pitfield, Milton Keynes, MK11 3LW, UK
UKHW022213310325
456962UK00007B/87